HTML5 and JavaScript Web Apps

Wesley Hales

Beijing · Cambridge · Farnham · Köln · Sebastopol · Tokyo

HTML5 and JavaScript Web Apps

by Wesley Hales

Published by O'Reilly Media, Inc., 1005 Gravenstein Highway North, Sebastopol, CA 95472.

O'Reilly books may be purchased for educational, business, or sales promotional use. Online editions are also available for most titles (*http://my.safaribooksonline.com*). For more information, contact our corporate/institutional sales department: 800-998-9938 or *corporate@oreilly.com*.

Editors: Simon St. Laurent and Meghan Blanchette	**Proofreader:** Linley Dolby
Production Editor: Christopher Hearse	**Indexer:** Meghan Jones
Copyeditor: Linda Laflamme	**Cover Designer:** Randy Comer
	Interior Designer: David Futato
	Illustrator: Rebecca Demarest

October 2012:   First Edition

Revision History for the First Edition:

2012-10-26   First release

See *http://oreilly.com/catalog/errata.csp?isbn=9781449320515* for release details.

ISBN: 978-1-449-32051-5

[LSI]

Table of Contents

Preface

HTML5 and JavaScript Web Apps is about building web applications with HTML5 and W3C specifications that are widely supported across all devices and browsers. It is intended for programmers who are facing the challenges of moving more code to the frontend with JavaScript, CSS, and HTML, while at the same time providing a backend infrastructure that is loosely coupled and supportive of offline clients.

My goal is to take you through, from beginning to end, each step of research and development for building a web application in today's new, brave world of mobile-first, responsive, progressive, and MVwhatever JavaScript-based applications. Each chapter contains real-world examples and uses of each specification discussed.

A few core W3C specifications are considered the cornerstones of today's "enterprise" web apps: Web Storage, Web Workers, Geolocation, Device Orientation, and Web Sockets. In the chapters that follow, you'll learn how to use these specifications in both mobile and desktop environments, as well as how to deal with fragmentation. Along the way, you'll also discover the hidden details and intricacies that you must know to create the most amazing application the universe has ever seen.

Many books describe the drama of what went down between the W3C and the WHATWG during the making of HTML5, and just as many people will tell you that "HTML5" is now only a marketing term. I agree to some extent, but that's only part of the story. The important things to understand, and the focus of this book, are the game-changing aspects and challenges of developing web applications with the specifications that have fallen under the HTML5 umbrella or just received attention with the rise of HTML5.

Who This Book Is For

The way we write web apps is changing—and it will always change. This book attempts to capture a snapshot in time of the HTML5 revolution and covers topics from beginner to advanced. Maybe you're a novice who's just starting to learn web application development, or maybe you're an expert fine-tuning your existing stack. Either way, *HTML5 and JavaScript Web Apps* will give you a baseline for building advanced client-side web applications.

If you're a developer aiming to write lightning-fast, HTML5-driven applications, as well as to understand how the server interacts with today's newer client-side concepts and technologies, then this book is for you.

Who This Book Is Not For

If you're just starting to learn JavaScript, CSS, or HTML, then this book is not for you. Consult one of the many books that cover the basics of web application development before you begin reading *HTML5 and JavaScript Web Apps*. This book assumes you understand how to build a web application and have written one before with such libraries as jQuery, Prototype, or plain old DOM APIs.

Also, if you are convinced that server-side generated markup is the way of the future, then chances are you won't enjoy this book. The topics covered here are mostly directed toward developers who think "offline first" and write modern web applications that start out *not* worrying about the server. The main idea driving this book is to use the web browser as a platform.

Finally, this book is geared toward the UI. There are a few examples of server-side code, mainly in Chapter 5, but everything else is client-side code with JavaScript and CSS.

What You'll Learn

The world of HTLM5 and mobile is moving at light speed, and we are witnessing a revolution and shift from traditional server-side concepts to heavier client-side ideas. In this environment, building a web app purely from HTML5 and related specifications is complicated and challenging, to say the least. These standards can adapt gracefully across mobile and desktop browsers, however, and this book will help you shoulder the challenge.

Chapter 1 and Chapter 2 start with an overview of the Mobile Web and will help you get a good grasp on which browsers support the standards that this book talks about and which browsers you should support. Here you'll learn on how to grade browsers so that your development team, QA team, and customers will know where you stand on browser support.

Chapter 3 jumps straight into developing a mobile web application with HTML5. This chapter will give you a starting point for building an application with native-like touch events and transitions. You'll also learn to add offline support with the AppCache and dynamically enhance your app based on the type of network the user is on (3G, WiFi, an so on).

Chapter 4 introduces you to concepts and features that apply to all browsers, both mobile and desktop. This chapter covers advanced server-side topics, such as compression and minification, along with frameworks that can help you develop a build process. This chapter also compares today's top five JavaScript MVC frameworks and how they interact with the server. Unlike other books that cover only the basics of JavaScript MVC, Chapter 4 takes a heavier look at how these frameworks interact with the server.

The remaining chapters go into detail on the five main HTML5 specifications. You'll learn about the raw implementation of each specification, as well as how it's used in real-world scenarios and use cases. Each chapter ends with a look at the frameworks available that support each technology.

For example, Chapter 5 takes a broad look at WebSockets and how you can use it on the client and server. This is the only chapter that goes into detail on server-side code. You'll set up a simple WebSocket server and compare frameworks that can be used across mobile and desktop browsers. The chapter also contains a detailed comparison of Socket.IO, Vert.x, and Atmosphere.

Chapter 6 goes into detail on Web Storage. You'll see how today's top sites like Google, Yahoo!, Twitter, and Amazon are storing data on the client side and investigate the best ways to store data along with a breakdown of available frameworks.

Next, Chapter 7 looks at Geolocation and discusses real-world uses of tracking users with mobile web browsers and other concepts. This chapter outlines how to use the technology and where you might encounter pitfalls in various implementations.

Chapter 8 covers the Device Orientation API. Although it's not the most glorious specification in existence, it has extremely valuable and valid uses, as you'll learn. This chapter ends with an implementation using orientation for page navigation on mobile devices.

Focused on Web Workers, Chapter 9 goes into practical uses of threading in the browser, delving into more detail than simply processing prime numbers in a separate thread. The chapter provides real-world examples of using Web Workers for processing image data and shows you how to create your own thread pool.

By the end of the book, you should be comfortable with writing your own HTML5 web app that works across any browsers you wish to support. You will have a true understanding of what you can build with HTML5, its available frameworks, and today's web browsers.

About the Code

The examples in this book are maintained at *http://github.com/html5e*. The JavaScript and CSS are self-contained in a simple framework called *slidfast.js* and *slidfast.css*. The JavaScript was purposely created to have no dependencies on any other libraries or frameworks. It is built specifically to showcase core JavaScript and DOM APIs that are provided by the browsers covered in each chapter. It's a learning framework not intended for public consumption, but by all means, learn from it and use it wherever you feel necessary.

Conventions Used in This Book

The following typographical conventions are used in this book:

Italic

   Indicates new terms, URLs, email addresses, filenames, and file extensions.

`Constant width`

   Used for program listings, as well as within paragraphs to refer to program elements such as variable or function names, databases, data types, environment variables, statements, and keywords.

`Constant width bold`

   Shows commands or other text that should be typed literally by the user.

`Constant width italic`

   Shows text that should be replaced with user-supplied values or by values determined by context.

   This icon signifies a tip, suggestion, or general note.

   This icon indicates a warning or caution.

Using Code Examples

This book is here to help you get your job done. In general, you may use the code in this book in your programs and documentation. You do not need to contact us for permission unless you're reproducing a significant portion of the code. For example, writing a program that uses several chunks of code from this book does not require permission.

Selling or distributing a CD-ROM of examples from O'Reilly books does require permission. Answering a question by citing this book and quoting example code does not require permission. Incorporating a significant amount of example code from this book into your product's documentation does require permission.

We appreciate, but do not require, attribution. An attribution usually includes the title, author, publisher, and ISBN. For example: "*HTML5 and JavaScript Web Apps* by Wesley Hales (O'Reilly). Copyright 2013 Hales Consulting, Inc., 978-1-449-32051-5."

If you feel your use of code examples falls outside fair use or the permission given above, feel free to contact us at *permissions@oreilly.com*.

Safari® Books Online

 Safari Books Online (*www.safaribooksonline.com*) is an on-demand digital library that delivers expert content in both book and video form from the world's leading authors in technology and business.

Technology professionals, software developers, web designers, and business and creative professionals use Safari Books Online as their primary resource for research, problem solving, learning, and certification training.

Safari Books Online offers a range of product mixes and pricing programs for organizations, government agencies, and individuals. Subscribers have access to thousands of books, training videos, and prepublication manuscripts in one fully searchable database from publishers like O'Reilly Media, Prentice Hall Professional, Addison-Wesley Professional, Microsoft Press, Sams, Que, Peachpit Press, Focal Press, Cisco Press, John Wiley & Sons, Syngress, Morgan Kaufmann, IBM Redbooks, Packt, Adobe Press, FT Press, Apress, Manning, New Riders, McGraw-Hill, Jones & Bartlett, Course Technology, and dozens more. For more information about Safari Books Online, please visit us online.

How to Contact Us

Please address comments and questions concerning this book to the publisher:

O'Reilly Media, Inc.
1005 Gravenstein Highway North
Sebastopol, CA 95472
800-998-9938 (in the United States or Canada)
707-829-0515 (international or local)
707-829-0104 (fax)

We have a web page for this book, where we list errata, examples, and any additional information. You can access this page here (*http://oreil.ly/HTML5-JS-Web-Apps*).

To comment or ask technical questions about this book, send email to *bookquestions@oreilly.com*.

For more information about our books, courses, conferences, and news, see our website at *http://www.oreilly.com*.

Find us on Facebook: *http://facebook.com/oreilly*

Follow us on Twitter: *http://twitter.com/oreillymedia*

Watch us on YouTube: *http://www.youtube.com/oreillymedia*

Acknowledgments

This book is dedicated to my incredible wife, Kristen, and our beautiful children, Adam and Stella. I also thank and dedicate this effort to Jesus Christ, who has given me the talent and ability to write this book.

The book would not have been possible without Meghan Blanchette and Simon St. Laurent continually pushing me to do better. I'm not a super easy guy to work with and can be quite lazy at times ☺, so they deserve serious props.

Also, many, many thanks to Douglas Campos, Brian Leroux, Divya Manian, Jason Porter, Shelley Powers, and Darren Nelsen for taking the time to review this book. I sought out the best developers, authors, and speakers in the industry to provide feedback, and they pushed me to places I did not think about. They gave me great perspective on the different aspects of HTML5 and today's Web. It was an honor to work with them and have their input.

Last but not least, the open source community around HTML5 and open web technologies is my source of inspiration, ideas, and fuel for this book. I would not be where I am today without the countless people who give so much back to the community from which they take. So thanks to you all.

## CHAPTER 1

Client-Side Architecture

Today, client-side development clearly requires more thought and investment in the architecture of HTML-driven applications. As web applications evolve, we are witnessing a serious shift from traditional server-side frameworks with tightly coupled templating logic and heavy backend processing to loosely coupled JavaScript clients that can go on- and offline at any time.

But is all of this just a repeat of the past? Haven't we already gone through the fat-client phases of the '80s and '90s, illustrated in Figure 1-1?

Figure 1-1. Fat clients used to be all the rage through the '80s and '90s

Unlike 20 years ago, browsers—the client-side platforms of today—are much more powerful, not to mention mobile. Plus, today's clients can report all kinds of interesting data, such as your location's latitude and longitude, through the browser and over a cell network.

One other small fact that's pushing the browser as a platform is that multiple companies —Google, Apple, Mozilla, and Microsoft—are pushing thousands of commits per week into improving their hybrid, thick-client technology platforms.

In the past, building applications that were heavily tied to the server made perfect sense. This gave hardcore, backend developers the freedom not to worry about DOM manipulation and CSS. If you could get a data grid or paging component that tied into your backend code and generated IE6- through IE8-compatible markup, then you were golden. (See Figure 1-2.)

Select		Cars	Color
⦿	1	Car Type 1	blue
○	1	Car Type 1	red
○	1	Car Type 1	green
○	1	Car Type 1	black
○	1	Car Type 1	white
○	2	Car Type 2	blue
○	2	Car Type 2	red
○	2	Car Type 2	green
○	2	Car Type 2	black
○	2	Car Type 2	white

First FRW Prev 1 2 3 4 5 Next FFW Last

Row number: 0 selected!

[Select]

Figure 1-2. Output of a JSF data grid component

This autogenerated markup comes at a cost, however, especially in today's world of fast moving, fragmented browsers. The need for flexible, controllable markup is at an all-time high. The Open Web is moving faster than ever, and user interfaces can no longer allow the server to be the bottleneck between stale ideas of the past and lightning-fast, scalable, frontend code. Developers have never been more concerned with performance in the browser. How markup is rendered and asynchronous resources are loaded can make or break your application. Faster and leaner frontends equal more lead conversions, better SEO rankings, and lower costs in the data center.

Before HTML5

Before HTML5 and mobile devices, frontend (or UI) developers didn't care that much about the architecture behind the user interface. The scene was full of hacks and proprietary plug-ins. Many developers focused on supporting browsers like IE6, Firefox, Safari, and maybe a few others. They wrote clean, semantic markup and worried about how valid their XHTML was. They imported the occasional JavaScript library to create some nice effects, and *prototype.js* or jQuery was the backbone (no pun intended) of the application.

Once developers worked around the browser quirks and bugs of a given application, things pretty much stayed the same. The architecture of advanced web applications was mostly managed on the server. Applications were dependent on how fast the incoming HTTP request could be handled and how fast markup could be rendered back to the user's web browser. With server-side templating and component frameworks, the server parsed the template and data was interlaced with regular XHTML or HTML markup. For Java, you might have used JSP, Velocity, Tiles, GWT, or JSF to achieve this. For Ruby, it was ERB, HAML, or RedCloth, and the list goes on. Every server-side web framework had an accompanying UI templating engine to go along with it or to choose from. This was the way of UI development for the past 10 years or more, and it probably will continue for a while yet. But it doesn't have to. The time has come to rethink how we build our new generation of web applications.

You might ask, "Why do we need to change the way in which our frontend is generated?" or "Why are we moving all our code to run inside the web browser and not on the server?" The first answer that comes to mind is that the web browser is becoming a platform. Our applications now live inside of platforms (or browsers) that are orders of magnitude more capable than their ancestors. Today's web applications are just that: they're apps. We're not creating sites anymore; we're creating robust applications with HTML5, CSS, and JavaScript at the core, as you can see in the HTML5 badge shown in Figure 1-3.

Figure 1-3. HTML5 badge

It's time to take a step back and look at how we're building our applications and level the client-side playing field. Developers must understand which frameworks and approaches are needed to build a scalable, rock-solid user interface for any given application.

More Code on the Client

The balance is undeniably moving from traditional server-side templating to JavaScript templating. With so many new JavaScript frameworks out there, we may seem to be going a little overboard, but this is what happens as technology shifts and then finds a decent balance. The technology that drives our UI is changing as browsers become more mobile and as they're given more hardware access through JavaScript APIs. To some degree, the concept of building a user interface remains the same across both client and server approaches. They all have data that needs to be presented and data that needs to be gathered. We're still adding framework-specific tags or attributes to our code so that the data knows where to be displayed, but the dependence on the server is gone. We are now getting objects and data back from intermittent RESTful or WebSocket connections, which are automatically bound to the UI through a client-side, JavaScript framework. Our applications now have the ability to occasionally sync data and the power to function offline.

To harness this power and to handle the different states of our applications, we must consider new approaches for managing client-side code. JavaScript libraries like jQuery and prototype must not define our frontend development models. Cross-browser DOM manipulation libraries should be taken very seriously, but the complexities of a scalable client-side architecture deserve much more attention than they have been given in the past. Organizing code and your application structure with mature techniques gathered from the classic *Design Patterns: Elements of Reusable Object-Oriented Software* (*http://en.wikipedia.org/wiki/Design_Patterns*) by Erich Gamma, et al., (Addison-Wesley Professional, 1995), is just the beginning. More than 40 MVC JavaScript frameworks now claim to be MVC, but they should be called *MV**. They all use different techniques for managing models, views, and controllers, and many seriously depart from the original Smalltalk MVC concepts. And even though JavaScript frameworks give us a nice way to organize and structure our code, we must deal with browser APIs that expose hardware-level access, such as Geolocation or Web Workers, on our own. The architecture of heavy, HTML5-driven user interfaces is still in its infancy, but fortunately you have this book to help light your path.

The Browser as a Platform

The web browser is becoming, or already is, an additional platform for our application stacks. It gets just as much, if not more, consideration than the server-side when choosing what our applications must support. Our frontend code is now packaged in native apps, extensions, and operating systems that are all driven by HTML5. As we are seeing with Google's Chrome OS and Mozilla's Boot 2 Gecko projects, the Open Web is very clearly being considered the platform for which web applications should and will be written.

HTML5, the Open Web, and mobile devices have helped push the browser-as-a-platform forward, giving browsers the capabilities of storing data and running applications in an offline state. But many of the newer standards driving this platform may not be finalized or implemented consistently across all the web browsers you wish to target.

The good thing is that there are workarounds in the majority of cases and browser vendors such as Microsoft, Opera, Google, Apple, and Mozilla are clearly taking the stance of providing a platform for developers with their respective browsers (see Figure 1-4).

Figure 1-4. Potential upcoming browser platforms

Conclusion

Whether you work for a large company or a budding startup, you must hone your skills, look past shiny home pages, look past top rankings on Hacker News or reddit, and make decisions that are valuable to your current project. You must set up and maintain work-flows for writing, testing, and debugging code and the frameworks you choose. These workflows may consist of many libraries and processes, from enforcing automatic IDE inspections with JSHint to testing your code with a minified, concatenated version of all the JavaScript contained within your application. Overall, it's incredibly valuable to understand and embrace the tools that will help you deliver an amazing web application or enhance an existing one.

The architecture of client-side applications is in its infancy. Tools and processes will get better over time, and JavaScript will be considered the assembly language of the Web. Until that day comes, however, we are the pioneers in this new age of frontend development. Now is the time to seize the opportunity: create applications that are perform-ant, are scalable, and take advantage of the latest specifications that the Web has to offer. It is time to move the Web forward and make it better.

## CHAPTER 2

The Mobile Web

Consumers are on track to buy one billion HTML5-capable mobile devices in 2013. Today, half of US adults own smartphones. This comprises 150 million people, and 28% of those consider mobile their primary way of accessing the Web. The ground swell of support for HTML5 applications over native ones is here, and today's developers are flipping their priorities to put mobile development first.

Even in large enterprise environments, mobile browser statistics are on the rise and starting to align with their desktop cousins. We are still faced, however, with the fact that one third of the Internet is using a version of Internet Explorer older than 9. Even more sobering, in some cases, these early IE users can make up two thirds of the visitors to our sites. This will get better over time, and desktop users will upgrade to newer versions and better browsers, but as we push the Web forward and create amazing applications across all browsers, we must also create a solid architecture that will account for all users and give them the best experience possible.

The capabilities of web browsers mean everything to the success of our web projects and products. Whether for fun, profit, or the overall betterment of mankind, it's important to understand how data should be served up for both desktop and mobile users. Finding the common ground across all browsers and figuring out which pieces should be used in the construction of today's web applications is the goal of this chapter.

The *Mobile Web* refers to browser-based applications created for mobile devices, such as smartphones or tablets, which can be connected wirelessly. Since 2008, the Web has shifted toward focusing on mobile browsers, which are delivering an overall better quality of life for today's web developers and users. However, this better quality of life is sometimes short lived once you start testing your new mobile web app on the myriad of devices and browsers. You may begin to wonder just what is supported and which HTML5 features you should use to build your app.

Whether you're an HTML5, W3C standards-loving, Open Web expert or just coming fresh off HTML 1, this chapter will equip you with the latest code, trends, and market research to guide you through making the right decision for your next web project. So what are you waiting for? Level up!

Mobile First

First, let's get our priorities straight. Prioritizing mobile design and development over the desktop was once laughable. In just a few years, the idea of "mobile first" has taken over, giving web developers a breath of fresh air in terms of HTML5-based APIs toward hardware access on mobile devices.

Apart from the obvious, here are multiple reasons for thinking mobile first:

- Developing sites for constrained devices and resolutions will force you to create more fluid and flexible content.
- Device features, such as accelerometer and geolocation hardware, present new business opportunities with technologies like Augmented Reality.
- Overall, mobile first requires you to think in a code-quality mindset. Today, it's required for developers to worry about things like battery life when doing hardware-accelerated animations with CSS. This quality of development not only brings better performing apps, but it also encourages you to focus on cleaner semantics.
- As you wean yourself off of desktop-focused web development, mobile browsers give you a glimpse into the future. This allows you to stay on the bleeding edge and in touch with new specifications and features.

Unfortunately the Mobile Web isn't write-once-run-anywhere yet. As specifications become final and features are implemented, interoperability will be achieved. In today's world of mobile browsers, however, we don't have a largely consistent implementation across all browsers. Even though new tablets and phones are constantly being released to achieve a consistent level of HTML5 implementation, we all know that we're stuck supporting the older, fragmented devices for a set amount of time. So, needless to say, such devices as the iPhone 3G and any device that hasn't upgraded past Android 4 will be the IE6s of this mobile era.

Deciding What to Support

As the mobile landscape exists today, we have multiple platforms and browsers to support. When you use HTML5's core APIs, you're bound to the features that are supported by your target device. So it's critical to understand where the mobile browser scene is today—and where it's headed.

Writing mobile web apps that span all platforms and all browsers can be a huge undertaking. Previously, web app developers didn't care if a desktop computer had a camera or accelerometer attached to it. The web applications of yesterday were not tied to the operating system and the capabilities of desktop hardware. Now, the Mobile Web adds another dimension of support to the apps we build, and the fragmentation across browsers and devices is mind-blowing. We must now create applications to be compatible across browsers, platforms, *and* devices. For example, Android's WebKit-based browser supported Web Workers in version 2.1, but later disabled support in version 2.2, 3.0, and 4.0. Then, support of Web Workers was fixed and turned back on in 4.1! Confusing, right? This is what I mean by another dimension of support or *fragmentation*. You're not only supporting browsers, but the operating system the browser is tied to as well.

How do you sort it all out? Not to worry, the remainder of the chapter examines the various mobile browsers, discusses the commonly supported APIs of each device, and identifies a core set of features from which you can build a solid enterprise mobile web app.

 You can find the latest matrix of HTML5 support across all rendering engines on the HTML5 engine comparison (*http://en.wikipedia.org/ wiki/Comparison_of_layout_engines_(HTML5)*) page on Wikipedia.

Mobile Web Browsers

Take a moment to review the various mobile browsers and their respective communities. As developers, we must try to embrace all platforms and develop applications that span all of the following browsers—and more if needed. For example, your users should not be limited to a WebKit-only mobile application in which your code runs on iOS and Android only.

WebKit

WebKit (*http://www.webkit.org*) is the browser engine behind Mobile Safari, Android, and Chrome, to name a few. This open source project is constantly pushing the open web envelope, adapting to the latest W3C specifications as they're published. The recent explosion of interest in WebKit can be attributed to the fact that it powers many of the leading mobile platform browsers.

Figure 2-1 shows the source code revision (vertical) as the function of time (horizontal). Some icons are there to represent products associated with WebKit; the position approximately resembles the era those products were made popular.

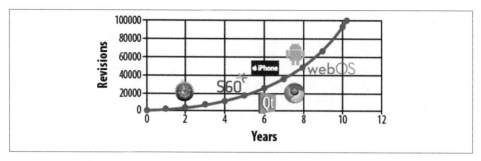

Figure 2-1. WebKit revisions

Mobile Safari (iOS6). Apple's adoption and implementation of early HTML5 specifications has been impressive. The company has been an obvious force in pushing the Web forward. With standard hardware and multicore technology, iPhones and iPads have been a great platform for HTML5 development. But, it's not all ponies and rainbows in iOS land, as each mobile browser has its share of quirks and bugs. Earlier iOS versions suffered from a bug with JavaScript's `innerHTML()` and forced developers to think of new ways to insert dynamic content. You'll see the solution to this problem in the next chapter—as for now, we'll focus on the big picture.

Apple's community process around iOS progression and filing bugs is bound and limited to the way Apple chooses to do things. You can file bugs with its BugReporter (*http://bugreport.apple.com*), but you can search through issues that you submit only. Luckily, once again, the community has stepped up to give Apple a hand in allowing nonconfidential data from customers to be openly searched. To see if your bug has already been filed, you can visit *http://openradar.appspot.com/faq*.

Android. Even though the Android default browser is based on WebKit, as of this writing, its implementation of HTML5 specifications is just starting to beef up in version 4. As Android evolves, we can rest assured that the coming HTML5 implementations will evolve with its community (*http://source.android.com/community*). For now, however, Android devices are horribly fragmented, and HTML5 support varies on devices and OS versions.

As for Android's future, the newer Dolphin browser (*http://dolphin-browser.com*) promises to deliver major advances in browser technology:

- 5 to 10 times faster than the default Android browser
- 100% faster than Chrome (at times)
- Scored over a 450 when tested on the respected test site, *http://HTML5test.com*, shown in Figure 2-2

		Score	Bonus
Dolphin Engine Beta »	Android 2.2 or higher	450	3
BlackBerry 10 »		447	10
Tizen 1 »		408	15
iOS 6.0 »	Apple iPhone, iPad and iPod Touch	360	9
Firefox Mobile 12 »	Multiple platforms	328	9
Windows Phone 8 »		300	6
Nokia Belle FP 2 » S60 5.5		256	9

Figure 2-2. Performance test results from http://html5test.com/results/mobile.html

Mobile Firefox

Mozilla has been around for a while and is stronger than ever in focusing on community efforts and pushing the Web forward. As of this writing, Mobile Firefox is in third place for the best HTML5 implementation (Figure 2-3) and has trumped Mobile Safari (iOS) in terms of implemented HTML5 features.

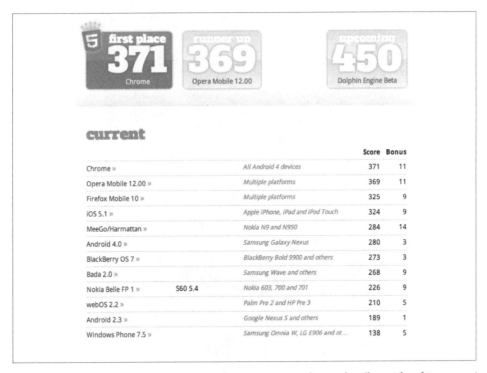

Figure 2-3. Best mobile HTML5 implementation with results (http://html5test.com/results-mobile.html)

This swapping of the throne will continue as the Mobile Web moves forward and evolves —and that's a good thing. We want competition and standards progression. Mozilla is no stranger to the evolution of the Mobile Web with its ambitious new project called WebAPI (*https://wiki.mozilla.org/WebAPI*). The WebAPI project is a set of APIs for accessing device functionality usually accessible only for native applications. In summary, it's an OS based on HTML, CSS, and JavaScript for mobile devices. It's yet another effort to move the Web forward and enable developers to write web applications once for all mobile operating systems. Estimated delivery for the WebAPI project is mid-2012 through the Boot to Gecko project (B2G). Figure 2-4 shows a screenshot of B2G's Gaia UI.

Figure 2-4. B2G's Gaia UI

Opera Mobile

Opera (*http://www.opera.com/mobile*) has two separate browsers for mobile phones: Opera Mobile and Opera Mini. In Opera Mini, the Opera Presto browser engine is located on a server. In Opera Mobile, it is installed on the phone. Currently, Opera Mini holds a large percentage of market share among other browsers, but for enterprise HTML5 applications, Opera Mobile supports the core specifications we need, such as Web Storage, Web Workers, and Geolocation.

Internet Explorer Mobile

Windows Phone 7.5 features a version of Internet Explorer Mobile with a rendering engine that is based on Internet Explorer 9. So the simplest way of explaining what Windows Phone supports is to say that it supports what IE9 supports, including Web Storage and Geo location. The supported specifications for IE9 Mobile can be found at *http://windowsteamblog.com/windows_phone/b/wpdev/archive/2011/09/22/ie9-mobile-developer-overview.aspx*.

On a better note, Windows Phone 8 supports IE10. Internet Explorer 10 includes much better support for such HTML5 features as WebSockets, Web Workers, Application Cache, and IndexedDB.

Mobile Browser Market Share

As of the latest worldwide report on browser market share, WebKit-based browsers are clearly in the lead with over 80% of the market (Figure 2-5). Right now, Android and iOS dominate, but as new operating systems, such as Mozilla's HTML5-based mobile B2G project, emerge we could see another shift of power in the ongoing "browser war."

Things are moving fast already. During the months that it took me to write this book, WebKit-based browsers grew from a 75% market share in October 2011 to more than 80% in 2012. Opera Mini shrunk from 18.65% to 12%. IE browsers grew from .16% to . 58%, but Microsoft is just starting up its marketing machine for the Windows Phone platform in 2012—so expect that IE number to grow.

 You can check the latest browser statistics at *http://www.netmarket share.com/browser-market-share.aspx?qprid=0&qpcustomd=1*.

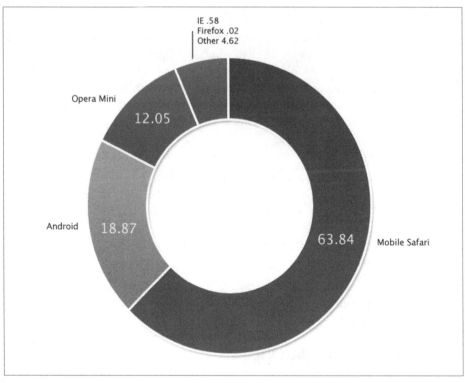

Figure 2-5. Worldwide market share by browser; May 2012 data provided by Net Applications (http://www.netapplications.com/)

Browser Grading

All of this information leads into the important topic of browser grading. Browser grading is a must for any mobile web project. It gives developers and QA a way to keep sane while developing and testing your application. It also sets forth a specific support schedule for your users and an overall target for your mobile web app's capabilities. Table 2-1 illustrates a sample browser grading sheet from QuirksMode (*http://www.quirks mode.org/blog/archives/2010/08/first_serious_s.html*).

Table 2-1. Browser grading example

Grade	Description
A: High Quality	A high-quality browser with notable market share. A must-target browser for a mobile web developer.
B: Medium Quality	Either a lower quality browser with high market share or a high-quality browser with low market share. Depending upon your capabilities, you should work to support these browsers, as well.
C: Low Quality	Typically an extremely low-quality browser with high market share. Generally not capable of running modern JavaScript or DOM code. This browser should be targeted, but may have access to limited features only.
F: Failing	A barely functioning browser. Pick and choose your support wisely.

HTML5 in the Enterprise

With a clearer picture of the mobile device and browser landscape, you next need to determine which W3C specifications the various browsers support and how you can use them today. In terms of enterprise development, certain client-side APIs are considered the advanced building blocks of today's mobile web applications: Geolocation, WebSocket, Web Storage, Device Orientation, and Web Workers. These are the specifications on last call from the W3C; close to finalized, they are stable (for the most part) and adopted in today's mobile browsers. Of course, you can find many other great specifications like the Media Capture API, which allows access to the device audio, video, and images, but this book tries to stay focused on specifications that are widely supported across all browsers today.

Table 2-2 details the support of the building-block APIs in the five leading or upcoming mobile platforms. All of these mobile browsers are considered grade A, B, or C. Throughout the book and at *http://html5e.org*, I will refer to this group of specifications and browsers as *HTML5 Enterprise* or *HTML5e* to easily identify and build upon the same specifications and browsers across mobile and desktop environments.

Table 2-2. HTML5 Enterprise (HTML5e) mobile support

Browser	Geolocation	WebSocket	Web Storage	Device Orientation	Web Workers
Mobile Safari	Yes	Yes	Yes	Yes	Yes
Android	Yes	No	Yes	Yes	No
Mobile IE	Yes	Yes[a]	Yes	No	Yes[a]
Opera Mobile	Yes	Mixed[b]	Yes	Mixed[c]	Yes
Mobile Firefox	Yes	Mixed[b]	Yes	Yes	Yes

[a] Mobile IE from Windows Phone 7.5 does not support these, but Windows 8 and above does.

[b] Both Mozilla and Opera have temporarily disabled WebSockets due to security issues with the protocol.

[c] Opera Mobile for Android has experimental support.

As you can see in Table 2-2, Mobile Firefox and Safari are the clear winners in terms of broad support, with Opera Mobile coming in at a close third. Android still has some work to do, and version 4 is looking much better. Likewise, Mobile IE has much better HTML5 support in IE10, but IE9 focused mainly on the "same markup" approach: trying to get things right in regard to HTML5-related markup and the IE rendering engine.

 For the latest browser HTML5 support information, check out *http://caniuse.com* and *http://mobilehtml5.org*.

Graceful Degradation

So you've decided which browsers you're going to support (all of them hopefully), but now you must *polyfill* or gracefully degrade, your apps where certain HTML5e specifications are not implemented. The premise for graceful degradation is to first build for the latest and greatest, then add *polyfills*, or handlers, for less capable devices. How can you create a development environment that will service your enterprise project needs and give you an API that works and degrades gracefully across multiple mobile browsers? At the end of each subsequent chapter, we'll look at approaches to handling these issues and identify projects that could possibly provide an open source solution.

You now have a starting point: a decent view of which HTML5 APIs are supported within mobile device browsers. In terms of the future, W3C, spec-driven, device features are only guaranteed to get better as new device operating systems are released and the specifications themselves become final. The following chapters will examine and rate available frameworks to form a reusable API for your project.

QA and Device Testing

In addition to deciding which browsers you are going to support, you need an easy way to develop and test across them. Enterprise development and QA cycles can get expensive depending on the scale of your project. So setting up the proper rapid development and testing environment is critical to success.

Because the current mobile market is mostly owned by Android and iOS, WebKit-based testing is fairly easy. You can test things out as you normally do on your desktop browser, then run them on a targeted mobile device that is backed by a version of WebKit. Just because you tested your app on the desktop version of Chrome or Safari, however, does not mean that everything will work properly across all WebKit-based mobile browsers. Nor does it mean that WebKit is the perfect representation of the Mobile Web. You should test across as many target platforms as possible based on W3C standards.

The best way to test your mobile HTML5-based application is to use the actual physical device you are targeting (or an emulator). As a service to developers, Max Firtman, the author of *Programming the Mobile Web* (O'Reilly) does a great job of identifying available emulators and maintains an up-to-date list, which you can find at mobilexweb (*http:// www.mobilexweb.com/emulators*) and preview in Figure 2-6.

Take a few moments to decide which emulator you may need and get ready for Chapter 3. There, you'll review how to debug hardware acceleration issues, investigate all the available remote debugging techniques, and learn how to work and develop across each browser.

Name	Official	Platform	Type	Browser testing	Native testing	Compatibility
iOS Simulator	Official	iOS	Simulator	Safari only	Objective-C	
Download	_**Devices**: iPhone 3GS, iPod Touch, iPhone 4, iPad (Tablet)_					
3.7Gb (login required)	Comes with XCode and Native SDK. You can't emulate Accelerometer/Gyroscope **(DeviceMotion API)**. You can't emulate URI-schemes, such as **click-to-call**. As a Simulator, it doesn't provide an AppStore; you can't install other browsers for testing, such as Opera Mini or Skyfire.					
Android Emulator	Official	Android	Emulator	Android Browser – others	Java	
Download	_**Devices**: Generic devices using 1.1, 1.5, 1.6, 2.0, 2.1, 2.2, 2.3, 3.0 O.S. platform_					
20Mb and 60Mb per platform package	We need to download images of the platforms after downloading the SDK. Look at **Chapter 4 of the book** for details. After downloading the platform, you can install **Firefox**, **Opera Mini**, **Opera Mobile**, **Skyfire** and **UCWEB** in your Android emulator for testing. You can download Motorola, Samsung and Nook add-ons (see below). Now it includes tablet support in HoneyComb (3.0)					
HP webOS Emulator	Official	webOS	Virtual Machine	webOS Browser	JavaScript – C++	
Download	_**Devices**: Palm Pre, Palm Pixi, Palm Pixi Plus_					
260Mb	Comes with SDK					
Samsung Galaxy Tab Add-on	Official	Android	Add-on	Android Browser – others	Java	
Download	_**Devices**: Samsung Galaxy Tab (Tablet)_					
52Mb	Requires Android SDK with 2.2 package. The download is done using the Android 2.3 SDK searching for third-party packages.					
Motorola						

Figure 2-6. List of emulators, available at mobilexweb (http://www.mobilexweb.com/emulators)

## CHAPTER 3

Building for the Mobile Web

The success of any mobile web application relies on two factors: design and performance. For mobile app design, we must have a consistent look and feel across all platforms. For better performance, we must have offline capabilities, animations on the UI, and back-end services that retrieve and send data via RESTful or WebSocket endpoints. To put it simply, your app is constrained by two ever-changing speeds: the speed of the device CPU/GPU and the speed of the Internet. The UI is handled by device hardware, such as the GPU, when doing native-like animations and transitions through CSS, and your backend services are limited to the current Internet connection speed of the mobile device.

In this chapter, we'll discuss how to design, create, and tune your mobile web app to be better looking and more performant. The chapter starts with a brief explanation of how apps should look for mobile devices then jumps into a low-level explanation of hardware-accelerated CSS and how to debug it. From there, you'll learn what it takes to build an offline mobile application and how to bring all the code together into one application to create a native-like mobile web app that is capable of handling intermittent Internet connections. Lastly, you'll examine today's most popular mobile frameworks to get an understanding of when or if you should add a community-supported framework to your project.

Mobile Web Look and Feel

The "native versus Mobile Web" debate isn't about which programming model will win. It's about what we can build until HTML5-like technologies catch up. We have three choices:

- Pure native approaches, which are clearly winning today in terms of overall application responsiveness

- Hybrid approaches and frameworks, which try to bridge the gap of HTML5 and native

- True, bleeding edge, mobile web frameworks, which are trying to conquer the native feel with markup, JavaScript, and CSS

Couple a fast and responsive mobile web app with your existing enterprise infrastructure, and let the games begin. Web standards are quickly closing the gap on missing native features, and device makers are catching up on implementing them. As of Android 3.1, for example, you can capture photos and videos due to the Media Capture API specification.

The W3C is a busy place these days, and developers are moving specifications and better use cases forward. Projects like jQuery are calling on the open source community to participate in these specifications and to submit their ideas for a better Web.

It only makes sense that mobile developers are leaning in favor of writing once, and running their app anywhere. *Write once, run anywhere*, or *WORA*, received a lot of fanfare after Sun's JVM started to emerge in the enterprise. With HTML5, WORA basically means you can use standard JavaScript and CSS to access all of the device features that a native application can (the device GPS, camera, accelerometer, etc.). This approach has given new life to browsers and a language (HTML) that was once only used to serve up documents—not apps.

The Look

To truly achieve that native look and feel, not only does your app need to respond quickly, but it must also look good. These days, the big secret to getting your native app listed in an App Store Top 10 list is to have a good-looking design. That's all it takes. If you have a killer data-driven application using all the latest device bells and whistles, it will not make it very far without a good clean design.

Overall, the Web has its own look and feel, and everyone knows that. There isn't a default look that will make all your users happy, however, so the burden is on you and your design team to create an attractive user experience.

iOS definitely has its own Mobile Web look and feel that mimics its native apps, but what about Android, Windows Mobile, Kindle, and all the other devices? Even if you could get your web app to respond like a native application, how do you conquer making it look like one? Because you are most concerned with only the three or four leading platforms, you could create three native skins for your target platforms and a default web look and feel for all the others.

Theresa Neil does a great job of explaining UI patterns for native apps in *Mobile Design Pattern Gallery* (O'Reilly). Her website (*http://www.mobiledesignpatterngallery.com/mobile-patterns.php*), (shown in Figure 3-1), is a great resource for trending patterns in mobile design.

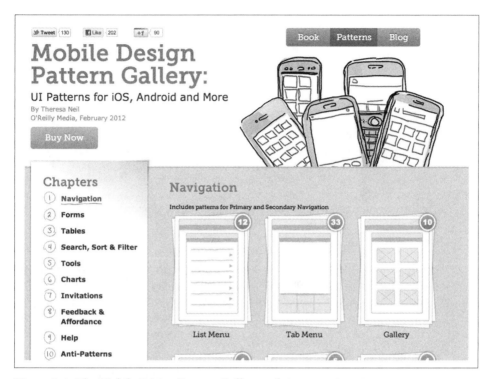

Figure 3-1. The Mobile Design Pattern Gallery website

The Feel

Spinning refreshes, choppy page transitions, and periodic delays in tap events are just a few of the headaches you face when attempting to create a mobile web app that behaves like a native one. Developers are trying to get as close to native as they possibly can, but are often derailed by hacks, resets, and rigid frameworks.

Hardware acceleration

Normally, GPUs handle detailed 3D modeling or CAD diagrams, but for mobile web apps, we want our primitive drawings (`div`s, backgrounds, text with drop shadows, images, etc.) to appear smooth and animate smoothly via the GPU. The unfortunate thing is that most frontend developers are dishing this animation process off to a third-party framework without being concerned about the semantics, but should these core CSS3 features be masked? Consider a few reasons why caring about hardware acceleration is important:

Memory allocation and computational burden
> If you go around compositing every element in the DOM just for the sake of hardware acceleration, the next person who works on your code may chase you down and beat you severely.

Power consumption and battery life
> Obviously, when hardware kicks in, so does the battery. Developers are forced to take the wide array of device constraints into consideration while writing mobile web apps. This will be even more prevalent as browser makers start to enable access to more and more device hardware. Luckily, we will soon have an API for checking the status of the device battery (*http://www.w3.org/TR/battery-status/*).

Conflicts
> You will encounter glitchy behavior when applying hardware acceleration to parts of the page that were already accelerated. So knowing if you have overlapping acceleration is *very* important.

To make user interaction smooth and as close to native as possible, you must make the browser work for you. Ideally, you want the mobile device CPU to set up the initial animation, and then have the GPU responsible for only compositing different layers during the animation process. This is what `translate3d`, `scale3d`, and `translateZ` do: they give the animated elements their own layer, thus allowing the device to render everything together smoothly.

CSS features can come at a cost on low-end devices. When using CSS `gradient`, `box-shadow`, `borders`, and `background-repeat`, you are using the device GPU to paint your images on the fly. CSS can be very powerful for rendering a nice user interface, but you should avoid doing this type of work in software when it can be prebaked in images. This means you should use sprites so the device downloads only a single image and embed data URIs in your CSS files for smaller images.

A few animations that don't require repaints are:

- `transition-property`
- `opacity`
- `transform`

CSS selector performance can cripple older mobile browsers. Using selectors like:

```
div[style*='foo']
```

will severely reduce performance on iOS devices up to version 4.3.x.

Interactions and Transitions

Take a look at three of the most common user-interaction approaches when developing a mobile web app: slide, flip, and rotation effects. First, we'll dissect the slide, flip, and rotation transitions and how they're accelerated. Notice how each animation requires only three or four lines of CSS and JavaScript. The examples don't use any additional frameworks, only DOM and vendor prefixed APIs.

 You can view this code in action at *http://html5e.org/example*. The demo is built for a mobile device, so fire up an emulator, use your phone or tablet, or reduce the size of your browser window to 1024px or less.

Sliding

The most common of the three approaches, sliding page transitions, mimics the native feel of mobile applications. The slide transition is invoked to bring a new content area into the view port.

For the slide effect, first you declare your markup:

```
<div id="home-page"
class="page">
  <h1>Home Page</h1>
</div>

<div id="products-page" class="page stage-right">
  <h1>Products Page</h1>
</div>

<div id="about-page" class="page stage-left">
  <h1>About Page</h1>
</div>
```

Notice that the pages are staged left and right. You could place them in any direction, but this is most common.

We now add animation plus hardware acceleration with just a few lines of CSS. The actual animation happens when we swap classes on the page div elements.

```
.page {
  position: absolute;
  width: 100%;
  height: 100%;
  /*activate the GPU for compositing each page */
  -webkit-transform: translate3d(0, 0, 0);
}
```

Although `translate3d(0,0,0)` is known as the silver bullet approach for WebKit, other browser engines like fennec (Mobile Firefox) and Opera Mobile do not support, or are just implementing, `translate3d` as of this writing. They do support 2D transformations, which cut out the Z-axis, so to support these browsers, you need to change:

```
transale3d(X,Y,Z);      // or
translateX(X), translateY(Y), translateZ(Z);
```

to:

```
translate(X,Y);
```

The one downside to 2D transforms is that, unlike 3D transforms, they are not GPU accelerated.

 Hardware acceleration tricks do not provide any speed improvement under Android Froyo 2.2 and beyond. All composition is done within the software.

When the user clicks a navigation element, we execute the following JavaScript (*https://github.com/html5e/slidfast/blob/master/slidfast.js#L319*) to swap the classes. We're not using any third-party frameworks yet, this is straight up JavaScript!

```
function slideTo(id) {
  //1.) the page we are bringing into focus dictates how
  // the current page will exit. So let's see what classes
  // our incoming page is using.
  //We know it will have stage[right|left|etc...]
  var classes = getElement(id).className.split(' ');

  //2.) decide if the incoming page is assigned to right or left
  // (-1 if no match)
  var stageType = classes.indexOf('stage-left');

  //3.) on initial page load focusPage is null, so we need
  // to set the default page which we're currently seeing.
  if (FOCUS_PAGE == null) {
    // use home page
    FOCUS_PAGE = getElement('home-page');
  }

  //4.) decide how this focused page should exit.
  if (stageType > 0) {
    FOCUS_PAGE.className = 'page transition stage-right';
  } else {
    FOCUS_PAGE.className = 'page transition stage-left';
  }

  //5. refresh/set the global variable
  FOCUS_PAGE = getElement(id);
```

```
//6. Bring in the new page.
FOCUS_PAGE.className = 'page transition stage-center';
}
```

`stage-left` or `stage-right` becomes `stage-center` and forces the page to slide into the center view port. We are completely depending on CSS3 to do the heavy lifting.

```
.stage-left {
  left: 100%;
}

.stage-right {
  left: 100%;
}

.stage-center {
  top: 0;
  left: 0;
}
```

By controlling the animations through swapping the `stage` classes in JavaScript, we are decoupling the CSS implementations from JavaScript. We could, however, control all the presentation logic within JavaScript by using:

```
FOCUS_PAGE.style.transform =
"translate(X,Y)";
```

Each browser vendor may be using a specific *vendor prefix* for the transform capabilities. One quick way of checking to see what your target browser supports is to use:

```
var getTransformProperty =
function(node) {
        var properties = [
                        'transform',
                        'WebkitTransform',
                        'msTransform',
                        'MozTransform',
                        'OTransform'
                ];
                var p;
                while (p = properties.shift()) {
                        if (typeof node.style[p] != 'undefined') {
                            document.
                            querySelector("#log").innerHTML += p + "<br/>";
                        }
                }
                return false;
        };
```

This slide effect has been tested on Mobile Safari, Android, Mobile Firefox (Figure 3-2), and Opera Mobile (Figure 3-3). You can also see the source code (*http://html5e.org*) that supports all the aforementioned browsers.

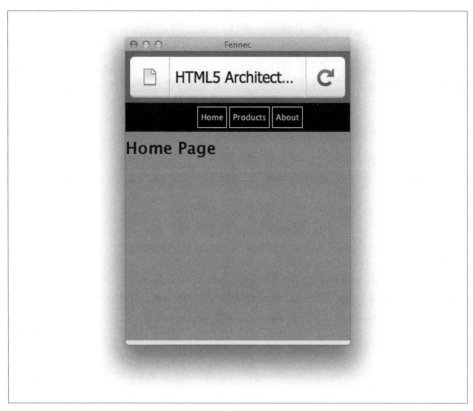

Figure 3-2. Slide transitions running on Mobile Firefox (Fennec)

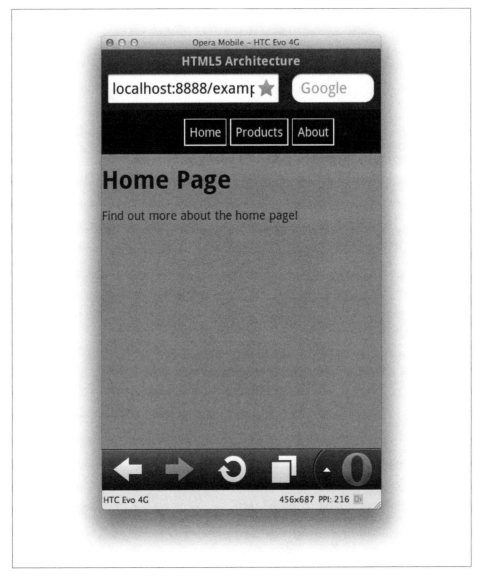

Figure 3-3. Slide transitions running on Opera Mobile 12

Flipping

On mobile devices, flipping is characterized by actually swiping the page away. Here you can use some simple JavaScript to handle the event on iOS and Android (WebKit-based) devices. Here is an example of flipping in action (*http://html5e.org/example/touch*) and the source (*https://github.com/html5e/slidfast/blob/master/slidfast.js#L411*) at github.

When dealing with touch events and transitions, the first thing you'll want is to get a handle on the current position of the element. Thanks to the CSSMatrix interface, which is implemented by WebKit only at the time of this writing, you can get an instance of WebKitCSSMatrix by passing the current transform's computed style.

```
function pageMove(event) {
  // get position after transform
  var curTransform =
  new WebKitCSSMatrix(window.getComputedStyle(page).webkitTransform);
  var pagePosition = curTransform.m41;
}
```

Because we are using a CSS3 ease-out transition for the page flip, the usual element.off setLeft will not work.

 For more information on WebKitCSSMatrix, go to Apple's developer page (http://bit.ly/apple-developer-webkitcss-matrix).

Next we want to figure out which direction the user is flipping and set a threshold for an event (page navigation) to take place.

```
if (pagePosition >= 0) {
 //moving current page to the right
 //so means we're flipping backwards
   if ((pagePosition > pageFlipThreshold) ||
          (swipeTime < swipeThreshold)) {
     //user wants to go backward
     slideDirection = 'right';
   } else {
     slideDirection = null;
   }
} else {
   //current page is sliding to the left
   if ((swipeTime < swipeThreshold) ||
          (pagePosition < pageFlipThreshold)) {
     //user wants to go forward
     slideDirection = 'left';
   } else {
     slideDirection = null;
   }
}
```

You'll also notice that we are measuring the swipeTime in milliseconds as well. This allows the navigation event to fire if the user quickly swipes the screen to turn a page.

To position the page and make the animations look native while a finger is touching the screen, we use CSS3 transitions after each event firing.

```
function positionPage(end) {
  page.style.webkitTransform = 'translate3d('+ currentPos + 'px, 0, 0)';
  if (end) {
    page.style.WebkitTransition = 'all .4s ease-out';
    //page.style.WebkitTransition = 'all .4s cubic-bezier(0,.58,.58,1)'
  } else {
    page.style.WebkitTransition = 'all .2s ease-out';
  }
```

For this example, `ease-out` did the trick, but for your own projects, play around with `cubic-bezier` to give the best native feel to your transitions.

Finally, to make the navigation happen, we must call the previously defined `slide To()` methods used in the last example.

```
track.ontouchend =
function(event) {
  pageMove(event);
  if (slideDirection == 'left') {
    slideTo('products-page');
  } else if (slideDirection == 'right') {
    slideTo('home-page');
  }
}
```

Rotating

Next, take a look at the rotate animation being used in this demo. At any time, you can rotate the page you're currently viewing 180 degrees to reveal the reverse side by tapping on the Contact menu option. Again, this only takes a few lines of CSS and some Java-Script to assign a transition class `onclick`.

 The rotate transition isn't rendered correctly on most versions of Android, because it lacks 3D CSS transform capabilities. Unfortunately, instead of ignoring the flip, Android makes the page "cartwheel" away by rotating instead of flipping. I recommend using this transition sparingly until support improves.

Here's the full source (*https://github.com/html5e/slidfast/blob/master/slidfast.js#L389*), but here's the markup (basic concept of front and back):

```
<div id="front"
class="normal">
...
</div>
<div id="back" class="flipped">
```

```
    <div id="contact-page" class="page">
        <h1>Contact Page</h1>
    </div>
</div>
```

The JavaScript you need is:

```
function flip(id) {
  // get a handle on the flippable region
  var front = getElement('front');
  var back = getElement('back');

  // again, just a simple way to see what the state is
  var classes = front.className.split(' ');
  var flipped = classes.indexOf('flipped');

  if (flipped >= 0) {
    // already flipped, so return to original
    front.className = 'normal';
    back.className = 'flipped';
    FLIPPED = false;
  } else {
    // do the flip
    front.className = 'flipped';
    back.className = 'normal';
    FLIPPED = true;
  }
}
```

Finally, here is the relevant CSS:

```
#back,
#front {
  position: absolute;
  width: 100%;
  height: 100%;
  -webkit-backface-visibility: hidden;
  -webkit-transition-duration: .5s;
  -webkit-transform-style: preserve-3d;
  -moz-backface-visibility: hidden;
  -moz-transform-style: preserve-3d;
  -moz-transition-duration: .5s;
}

.normal {
  -webkit-transform: rotateY(0deg);
  -moz-transform:  rotateY(0deg);
}

.flipped {
  -webkit-user-select: element;
  -webkit-transform: rotateY(180deg);
  -moz-transform:  rotateY(180deg);
}
```

Debugging Hardware Acceleration

With the code of the basic transitions covered, take a look at the mechanics of how the transitions run on the device and are composited. Here are a few tips to remember when using accelerated compositing:

- Reduce the quantity of layers
- Keep layers as small as possible
- Update layers infrequently
- Tailor layer compositing to your purpose
- Use trial and error; testing is important

To begin debugging, fire up a couple of WebKit-based browsers and your IDE of choice.

Using Safari

First, start Safari from the command line to make use of some debugging environment variables. I use a Mac, so the example commands might differ from those for your OS. Open the Terminal, and type the following (or just skip Safari and use the Chrome settings in next section):

```
$> export CA_COLOR_OPAQUE=1
$> export CA_LOG_MEMORY_USAGE=1
$> /Applications/Safari.app/Contents/MacOS/Safari
```

These lines start Safari with a couple of debugging helpers. CA_COLOR_OPAQUE shows you which elements are actually composited or accelerated, while CA_LOG_MEMORY_USAGE shows you how much memory you are using when sending drawing operations to the backing store. This tells you exactly how much strain you are putting on the mobile device and possibly give hints to how your GPU usage might be draining the target device's battery.

You may also start Safari after running the following command, which gives you a full Debug menu with all available options, as shown in Figure 3-4:

```
defaults write com.apple.Safari
IncludeInternalDebugMenu 1
```

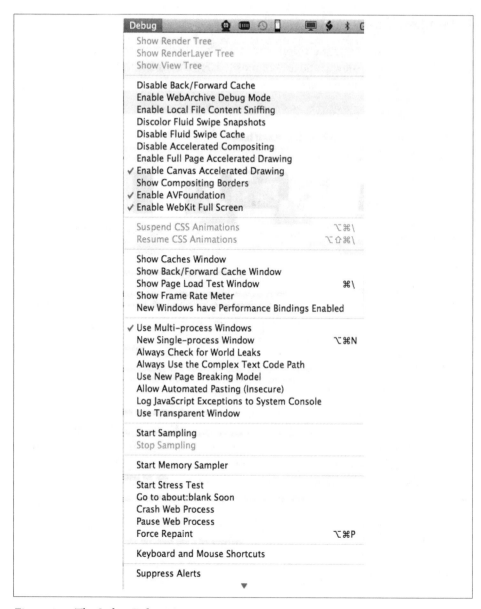

Figure 3-4. The Safari Debug menu

Using Chrome

Now fire up Chrome to see some good frames per second (FPS) information and borders around the composited layers:

1. Open the Google Chrome web browser.

2. In the URL bar, type **about:flags**.

3. Scroll down a few items, and click Enable for the FPS counter as shown in Figure 3-5.

Figure 3-5. The Chrome about:flags tab

 Do not enable the "GPU compositing on all pages" option. The FPS counter appears in the left corner only if the browser detects compositing in your markup—and that is what you want in this case.

If you view this page in your souped-up version of Chrome, you will see the red FPS counter in the top-left corner, as shown in Figure 3-6.

Figure 3-6. The Chrome FPS meter

This is how you know hardware acceleration is turned on. It also gives you an idea of how the animation runs and whether you have any leaks (continuous running animations that should be stopped).

Another way to visualize the hardware acceleration is to open the same page in Safari with the environment variables mentioned above. Every accelerated DOM element will have a red tint to it. This shows you exactly what is being composited by each layer, or accelerated div element. Notice in Figure 3-7, the white navigation is not red because it is not accelerated.

Figure 3-7. Debugging acceleration of the demo app

A similar setting for Chrome is also available in the about:flags tab: Click Enable for "Composited render layer borders."

Another great way to see an example of composited layers is to view the WebKit falling leaves demo (*http://www.webkit.org/blog-files/leaves/*) while CA_COLOR_OPAQUE=1 is applied. Figure 3-8 shows the results.

Figure 3-8. WebKit's Falling Leaves demo

Memory Consumption

Finally, to truly understand the graphics hardware performance of an application, look at how memory is being consumed. Here you can see that the app is pushing 1.38MB of drawing instructions to the CoreAnimation buffers on Mac OS. The CoreAnimation memory buffers are shared between OpenGL ES and the GPU to create the final pixels you see on the screen (Figure 3-9).

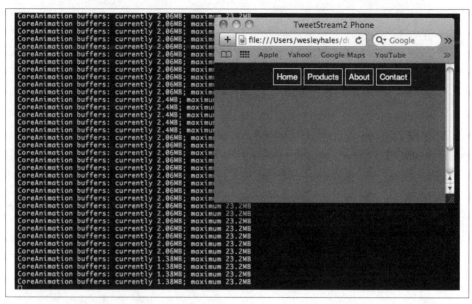

Figure 3-9. CoreAnimation debug session (small screen)

When you simply resize or maximize the browser window, you can see the memory expand as well (Figure 3-10).

Using the previous debugging techniques gives you an idea of how memory is being consumed on your mobile device only if you resize the browser to the correct dimensions. When debugging or testing for iPhone environments, for example, resize to 480 by 320 pixels.

This section illustrated how hardware acceleration works and what it takes to debug memory issues or other hardware accelerated glitches. It's one thing to read about it, but to actually see the GPU memory buffers working visually really brings things into perspective.

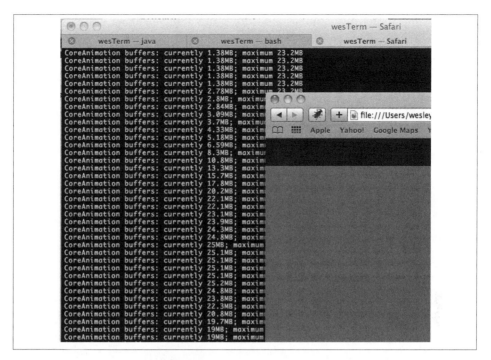

Figure 3-10. CoreAnimation debug session (enlarged screen)

Fetching and Caching

Now it's time to take your page and resource caching to the next level. Much like the approach that jQuery Mobile and similar frameworks use, you can prefetch and cache your pages with concurrent AJAX calls. A few core mobile web challenges highlight the reasons why following this approach makes sense:

Fetching

Prefetching your pages allows users to take the app offline and also eliminates waiting between navigation actions. Of course, you don't want to choke the device's bandwidth when the device comes online, so you need to use this feature sparingly.

Caching

You want a concurrent or asynchronous approach when fetching and caching pages. Because it's well supported among devices, you also need to use `localStorage`, which unfortunately isn't asynchronous.

AJAX and parsing the response

Using `innerHTML()` to insert the AJAX response into the DOM is dangerous, and it could be unreliable according to *http://martinkou.blogspot.com/2011/05/alternative-workaround-for-mobile.html*. Instead, I recommend a reliable mechanism for AJAX response insertion and handling concurrent calls (*https://community.jboss.org/people/wesleyhales/blog/2011/08/28/fixing-ajax-on-mobile-devices*). You also can leverage some new features of HTML5 for parsing the `xhr.re` `sponseText`.

You can build on the code from the slide, flip, and rotate demos by adding some secondary pages and linking to them. You can then parse the links and create transitions on the fly.

```
<div id="home-page"
class="page">
  <h1>Home Page</h1>
  <a href="demo2/home-detail.html" class="fetch">
      Find out more about the home page!
  </a>
</div>
```

As you can see, this snippet leverages semantic markup with a link to another page. The child page follows the same node/class structure as its parent. You could take this a step further and use the `data-*` attribute for `page` nodes, and the like.

Here is the detail page (child) located in a separate HTML file (*/demo2/home-detail.html*), which will be loaded, cached, and set up for transition on app load.

```
<div id="home-page-detail"
class="page">
    <h1>Home Page Details</h1>
    <p>Here are the details.</p>
</div>
```

Now take a look at the JavaScript. For simplicity's sake, I'm leaving any helpers or optimizations out of the code. The code is looping through a specified array of DOM nodes to dig out links to fetch and cache. For the complete source, see *https://github.com/html5e/slidfast/blob/master/slidfast.js#L264*.

```
var fetchAndCache = function()
{
  // iterate through all nodes in this DOM to
  //find all mobile pages we care about
  var pages = document.getElementsByClassName('page');

  for (var i = 0; i < pages.length; i++) {
    // find all links
    var pageLinks = pages[i].getElementsByTagName('a');

    for (var j = 0; j < pageLinks.length; j++) {
      var link = pageLinks[j];

      if (link.hasAttribute('href') &&
      //'#' in the href tells us that this page is
      //already loaded in the DOM - and
```

```
        // that it links to a mobile transition/page
          !(/[\#]/g).test(link.href) &&
        //check for an explicit class name setting to fetch this link
        (link.className.indexOf('fetch') >= 0))  {
        //fetch each url concurrently
        var ai = new ajax(link,function(text,url){
            //insert the new mobile page into the DOM
          insertPages(text,url);
        });
        ai.doGet();
      }
    }
  }
};
```

The use of the AJAX object ensures proper asynchronous post-processing. In this example, you see the basic use of caching on each request and of providing the cached objects when the server returns anything but a successful (200) response.

```
function processRequest () {
  if (req.readyState == 4) {
    if (req.status == 200) {
      if (supports_local_storage()) {
        localStorage[url] = req.responseText;
      }
      if (callback) callback(req.responseText,url);
    } else {
      // There is an error of some kind, use our
      //cached copy (if available).
      if (!!localStorage[url]) {
        // We have some data cached, return that to the callback.
        callback(localStorage[url],url);
        return;
      }
    }
  }
}
```

Unfortunately, because localStorage uses UTF-16 for character encoding, each single byte is stored as 2 bytes, bringing our storage limit from 5MB to 2.6MB total. Fetching and caching these pages/markup outside of the application cache scope allows you to take advantage of all the storage space provided by the device.

With the recent advances in the iframe element with HTML5, you now have a simple and effective way to parse the responseText you get back from an AJAX call. There are plenty of 3,000-line JavaScript parsers and regular expressions that remove script tags and so on. But why not let the browser do what it does best? The next example writes the responseText into a temporary hidden iframe. This uses the HTML5 sandbox attribute, which disables scripts and offers many security features. (See complete source (*https://github.com/html5e/slidfast/blob/master/slidfast.js#L191*).)

To quote the HTML5 spec: "The sandbox attribute, when specified, enables a set of extra restrictions on any content hosted by the iframe. Its value must be an unordered set of unique space-separated tokens that are ASCII case-insensitive. The allowed values are allow-forms, allow-same-origin, allow-scripts, and allow-top-navigation. When the attribute is set, the content is treated as being from a unique origin, forms and scripts are disabled, links are prevented from targeting other browsing contexts, and plug-ins are disabled. To limit the damage that can be caused by hostile HTML content, it should be served using the text/html-sandboxed MIME type."

```
var getFrame = function() {
    var frame = document.getElementById("temp-frame");

    if (!frame) {
        // create frame
        frame = document.createElement("iframe");
        frame.setAttribute("id", "temp-frame");
        frame.setAttribute("name", "temp-frame");
        frame.setAttribute("seamless", "");
        frame.setAttribute("sandbox", "allow-same-origin");
        frame.style.display = 'none';
        document.documentElement.appendChild(frame);
    }
    // load a page
    return frame.contentDocument;
};

var insertPages = function(text, originalLink) {
  var frame = getFrame();
  //write the ajax response text to the frame and let
  //the browser do the work
  frame.write(text);

  //now we have a DOM to work with
  var incomingPages = frame.getElementsByClassName('page');

  var pageCount = incomingPages.length;
  for (var i = 0; i < pageCount; i++) {
    //the new page will always be at index 0 because
    //the last one just got popped off the stack with
    //appendChild (below)
    var newPage = incomingPages[0];

    //stage the new pages to the left by default
    newPage.className = 'page stage-left';

    //find out where to insert
    var location = newPage.parentNode.id ==
```

```
                                'back' ? 'back' : 'front';

     try {
       // mobile safari will not allow nodes to be transferred from one
       // DOM to another so we must use adoptNode()
       document.getElementById(location).
                    appendChild(document.adoptNode(newPage));
     } catch(e) {
       // todo graceful degradation?
     }
   }
 };
```

The target browser (Mobile Safari) correctly refuses to implicitly move a node from one document to another. An error is raised if the new child node was created in a different document. So this example uses adoptNode, and all is well.

So why iframe? Why not just use innerHTML? Even though innerHTML is now part of the HTML5 spec, it is a dangerous practice to insert the response from a server (evil or good) into an unchecked area. innerHTML has also been noted to fail intermittently on iOS (just do a Google search on "ios innerhtml" to see the latest results) so it's best to have a good workaround when the time comes.

Figure 3-11 shows the latest performance test from *http://jsperf.com/ajax-response-handling-innerhtml-vs-sandboxed-iframe*. It shows that this sandboxed iframe approach is just as fast, if not faster than innerHTML on many of today's top mobile browsers. Keep in mind the measurement is operations per second, so higher scores are better.

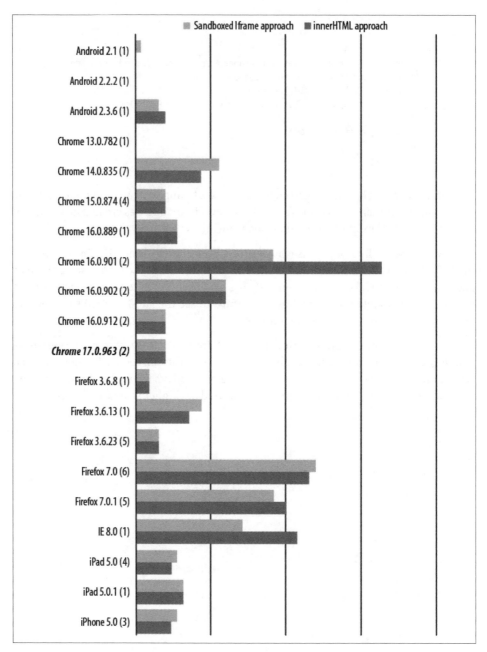

Figure 3-11. HTML5 iframe versus innerHTML() performance

Network Type Detection and Handling

Now that we have the ability to buffer (or predictive cache) the example web app, we must provide the proper connection detection features to make the app smarter. This is where mobile app development gets extremely sensitive to online/offline modes and connection speed. Enter the Network Information API. With it, you can set up an extremely smart mobile web app.

When would this be useful? Suppose someone on a high-speed train is using your app to interact with the Web. As the train rushes along, the network may very well go away at various moments, and various locales may support different transmission speeds (HSPA or 3G might be available in some urban areas, while remote areas might support much slower 2G technologies only). Not only does the following code address connection scenarios like this, it also:

- Provides offline access through `applicationCache`
- Detects if bookmarked and offline
- Detects when switching from offline to online and vice versa
- Detects slow connections and fetches content based on network type

Again, all of these features require very little code. The first step is detect the events and loading scenarios (see *https://github.com/html5e/slidfast/blob/master/slidfast.js#L536*):

```
window.addEventListener('load', function(e) {
 if (navigator.onLine) {
  // new page load
  processOnline();
 } else {
  // the app is probably already cached and (maybe) bookmarked...
  processOffline();
 }
}, false);

window.addEventListener("offline", function(e) {
  // we just lost our connection and entered offline mode,
  // disable external link
  processOffline(e.type);
}, false);

window.addEventListener("online", function(e) {
  // just came back online, enable links
  processOnline(e.type);
}, false);
```

In the `EventListener` statements above, we must tell the code if it is being called from an event or an actual page request or refresh. The main reason is because the `body` `onload` event won't be fired when switching between the online and offline modes.

The simple check for an `online` or `onload` event below resets disabled links when switching from offline to online. For a more sophisticated app, you could also insert logic that would resume fetching content or handle the UX for intermittent connections.

```
function
processOnline(eventType) {

  setupApp();
  checkAppCache();

  // reset our once disabled offline links
  if (eventType) {
    for (var i = 0; i < disabledLinks.length; i++) {
      disabledLinks[i].onclick = null;
    }
  }
}
```

For the `processOffline()` function, you could manipulate your app for offline mode and try to recover any transactions that were going on behind the scenes. The code below crawls the DOM for all of the external links and disables them, trapping users in our offline app—*forever*!

```
function processOffline() {
  setupApp();

  // disable external links until we come back
  // setting the bounds of app
  disabledLinks = getUnconvertedLinks(document);

  // helper for onlcick below
  var onclickHelper = function(e) {
    return function(f) {
      alert('This app is currently offline and cannot access the hotness');
      return false;
    }
  };

  for (var i = 0; i < disabledLinks.length; i++) {
    if (disabledLinks[i].onclick == null) {
      //alert user we're not online
      disabledLinks[i].onclick = onclickHelper(disabledLinks[i].href);

    }
  }
}
```

Okay, suppress your evil genius laugh, and let's get on to the good stuff. Now that the app knows what connected state it's in, we can also check the type of connection when it's online and adjust accordingly with the code below. In the comments, I listed typical North American providers' download and latencies for each connection.

```
function setupApp(){
  // create a custom object if navigator.connection isn't available
  var connection = navigator.connection || {'type':'0'};
  if (connection.type == 2 || connection.type == 1) {
      //wifi/ethernet
      //Coffee Wifi latency: ~75ms-200ms
      //Home Wifi latency: ~25-35ms
      //Coffee Wifi DL speed: ~550kbps-650kbps
      //Home Wifi DL speed: ~1000kbps-2000kbps
      fetchAndCache(true);
  } else if (connection.type == 3) {
  //edge
      //ATT Edge latency: ~400-600ms
      //ATT Edge DL speed: ~2-10kbps
      fetchAndCache(false);
  } else if (connection.type == 2) {
      //3g
      //ATT 3G latency: ~400ms
      //Verizon 3G latency: ~150-250ms
      //ATT 3G DL speed: ~60-100kbps
      //Verizon 3G DL speed: ~20-70kbps
      fetchAndCache(false);
  } else {
  //unknown
      fetchAndCache(true);
  }
}
```

There are numerous adjustments you could make to the fetchAndCache process, but
the example code simply tells it to fetch the resources asynchronous (true) or synchronous (false) for a given connection. To see how this works in practice, consider the edge
(synchronous) request timeline shown in Figure 3-12 and the WiFi (asynchronous) request timeline shown in Figure 3-13.

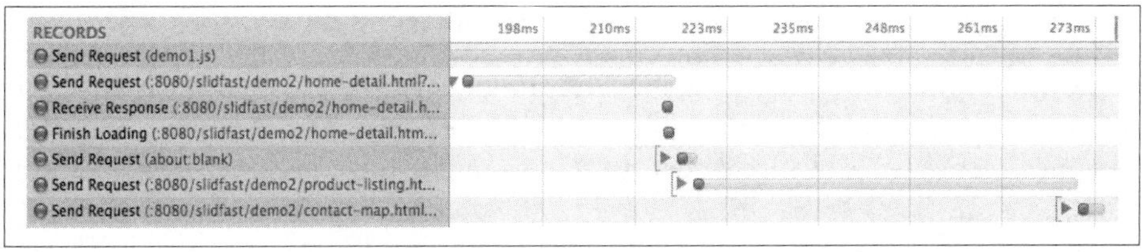

Figure 3-12. Synchronous page loading timeline

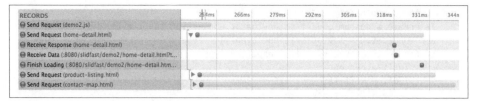

Figure 3-13. Asynchronous page loading timeline

The example code allows for at least some method of user experience adjustment based on slow or fast connections, but it is by no means an end-all-be-all solution. Another improvement would be to throw up a loading modal when a link is clicked (on slow connections) while the app still may be fetching that link's page in the background. Your overall goal is to cut down on latencies while leveraging the full capabilities of the user's connection with the latest and greatest HTML5 has to offer. You can view the network detection demo at *http://html5e.org/example*.

Frameworks and Approaches

It seems like there's a new JavaScript-based mobile framework popping up every day. You can literally spend days (or months) comparing frameworks and whipping up multiple proofs-of-concept (POCs), only to find out that you may not want or need a framework at all.

In the majority of situations, whether converting an existing app or starting from scratch, you're better off writing your own CSS and DOM interactions. The harder you lean on a framework, the harder your app will fall when problems arise. Knowing the basics and how to fix those problems under the hood are essential. The DOM is the underlying infrastructure and API for all web apps. No matter how much you like or dislike the API, if you desire a mobile web app that screams at blazing fast speeds and gets "close to the metal," you must understand how to work with it.

One commonly used programming model for the Mobile Web is called *single page*. This means you put your entire markup into a single HTML page, often enclosed by a `<div>` or some other sensible block element, as in this sample single-page web app structure:

```
<!DOCTYPE html>
<html lang="en" dir="ltr">
  <body>

    <div id="home-page">
      ...page content
    </div>

    <div id="contact-page">
      ...page content
```

```
    </div>

  </body>
</html>
```

Why put everything in one page? Primarily, it buys you native-like transitions and fewer initial HTTP requests. You must use AJAX and CSS3 transitions to emulate the feel of a native application and load data dynamically. This single-page approach also promotes including all your resources, such as JavaScript and CSS, within the file. Again, this reduces additional HTTP requests to get the best performance possible from your mobile application.

With an understanding of the basics, consider a few mobile-focused JavaScript frameworks that try to take care of the heavy lifting on the UI. Most of today's JavaScript frameworks have a specific browser or platform they're targeting. Some are WebKit-only and others try to span all device browsers. There may be features you need, and ones you don't. So it's up to you to decide when to bring any framework into your current or existing project.

 Some mobile frameworks extend or build on older, bloated, desktop-browser frameworks. Be careful that whichever framework you choose does not check for older IE6 bugs or platforms that you aren't targeting. This bloat may seem minimal to some, but as you will see in the next chapter, every byte you can shave off the initial load time will greatly enhance the user experience.

When evaluating mobile JavaScript frameworks, look for:

- Optimization for touch screen devices; make sure the framework uses CSS3 transitions to handle animations
- Cross-platform consistency across all the major platform (Grade A and B) browsers
- Use (or wrapping) of the latest HTML5 and CSS3 standards
- Strong open source community behind the framework

Finally, investigate the programming model uses and ask yourself: does my project require a dynamically generated UI through JavaScript, or do I want to declare my markup beforehand in the single-page approach?

The framework smackdown in the following sections provides an overview of the three main approaches to mobile web apps development: single page, no page structure, and 100% JavaScript-driven.

Single Page

As previously mentioned, the single-page approach forces you to put as much markup and resources as possible into a single HTML file. In the end, this limits HTTP requests for a better performing app. The leaders here are jQuery Mobile and jQTouch.

jQuery Mobile

jQuery Mobile (*http://jquerymobile.com*; demo at *http://jquerymobile.com/test*) is strictly tied to the release schedule of the core jQuery library. Known for its AJAX-based navigation system and themeable ThemeRoller designs, the framework is produced by the core jQuery project. It also has an attractive set of widgets, but unfortunately, they're all decorated with CSS background gradients, text shadows, rounded corners, and drop shadows. As you'll see in the coming chapters, heavy use of CSS decorations in mobile web apps can slow the browser to a crawl.

jQuery Mobile is the most popular mobile web framework out there today. Taking into account its over 10,000 followers on Twitter and more than 6,000 watchers on github (Figure 3-14), you can easily see the power piggy-backing on an existing project's success (in this case, core jQuery) to catapult a project into the mainstream. The real power and strength of this project comes from its community. Table 3-1 gives a high-level snapshot of the jQuery Mobile project.

Figure 3-14. jQuery Mobile github stats, June 2012

Table 3-1. jQuery Mobile

Platform support	Android, bada, BlackBerry, iOS, MeeGo, Symbian, webOS, and Windows Phone (others are graded at different levels of 49 support)
License	Dual license MIT or GPL 2
Programming model	CSS and JavaScript: declarative on the DOM itself; markup with CSS and data-* attributes
Wrapped or polyfilled HTML5 APIs	None

To set up the page, use the code:

```
<!DOCTYPE html>
<html>
    <head>
    <title>My Page</title>
    <meta name="viewport" content="width=device-width, initial-scale=1">
    <link rel="stylesheet" href="/jquery.mobile-1.0.min.css" />
    <script type="text/javascript" src="/jquery-1.6.4.min.js"></script>
    <script type="text/javascript" src=" /jquery.mobile-1.0.min.js"></script>
```

```
</head>
<body>

<div data-role="page">

    <div data-role="header">
        <h1>My Title</h1>
    </div><!-- /header -->

    <div data-role="content">
        <p>Hello world</p>
    </div><!-- /content -->

</div><!-- /page -->

</body>
</html>
```

To set up a component such as the one shown in Figure 3-15, use:

```
<ul data-role="listview"
data-inset="true" data-filter="true">
    <li><a href="#">Acura</a></li>
    <li><a href="#">Audi</a></li>
    <li><a href="#">BMW</a></li>
    <li><a href="#">Cadillac</a></li>
    <li><a href="#">Ferrari</a></li>
</ul>
```

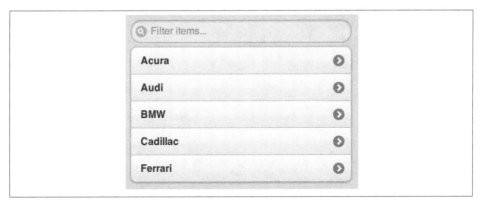

Figure 3-15. jQuery Mobile List View component

jQTouch

jQTouch (*http://jqtouch.com*) is a Zepto/jQuery plug-in and a good, simple framework to get started with quickly. It offers a basic set of widgets and animations but lacks support for multiple platforms. The framework also suffers from slow, flickering animations and delayed tap events. Supporting only iOS and Android, jQTouch is the second most popular framework on the interwebs with more than 9,000 Twitter followers and a nice following on github (Figure 3-16). However, the commit history in github looks a little sparse, with six-month gaps at times. Table 3-2 outlines its features. (Check out the jQTouch demo (*http://www.jqtouch.com/preview/demos/main*).)

Figure 3-16. jQTouch github stats, June 2012

Table 3-2. jQTouch

Platform support	Android and iOS only
License	MIT
Programming model	Heavy CSS, light JavaScript; uses CSS classes for detecting the appropriate animations and interactions; extensions supported
Wrapped or polyfilled HTML5 APIs	None

To set up the page, use the code:

```
<html>
    <head>
        <Title>My App</title>
    </head>
    <body>
        <div id="home">
            <div class="toolbar">
                <H1>Hello World</h1>
            </div>
            <ul class="edgetoedge">
                <li class="arrow"><a href="#item1">Item 1</a></li>
            </ul>
        </div>
    </body>
</html>
```

To set up the component shown in Figure 3-17, use:

```
<ul class="edgetoedge">
        <li class="arrow"><a id="0" href="#date">Today</a></li>
        <li class="arrow"><a id="1"
href="#date">Yesterday</a></li>
        <li class="arrow"><a id="2" href="#date">2 Days
Ago</a></li>
        <li class="arrow"><a id="3" href="#date">3 Days
Ago</a></li>
        <li class="arrow"><a id="4" href="#date">4 Days
```

```
Ago</a></li>
        <li class="arrow"><a id="5" href="#date">5 Days
Ago</a></li>
    </ul>
```

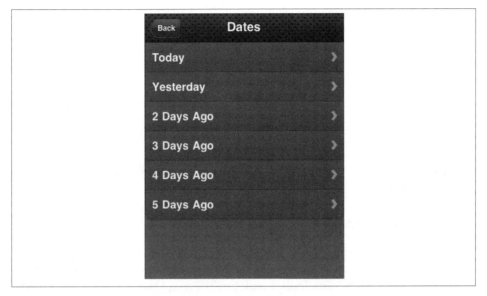

Figure 3-17. jQTouch List View component

No Page Structure

In the no-page-structure approach, the markup is flexible and lightweight. Unlike the single-page approach, markup here is not tied to a specific DOM structure. Your best option for using this method is xui.

xui

Born from the PhoneGap framework, xui (*http://xuijs.com*) does not try and dictate a page structure or widget paradigm. Instead, xui handles events, animations, transforms, and AJAX. It prides itself in being lightweight with the ability to add plug-ins for needed features.

xui is specifically tailored for DOM manipulation in a mobile environment. This is an important factor when dealing with existing desktop browser based frameworks like jQuery. With xui, you get a 10kb JavaScript file that gives you a very useful programming model. Brian Leroux is the author of xui and is well known within the HTML5/Open Web community. One notable thing about this project is the all-star list of contributors to the code: Rebecca Murphey, Remy Sharp, Fil Maj, Alex Sexton, Joe McCann, and many others. So, point being, sometimes it helps to judge a project's value by who the contributors and founders are opposed to how many followers it has (Figure 3-18). Table 3-3 outlines its stats.

Figure 3-18. xui github stats, June 2012

Table 3-3. xui

Platform support	WebKit, IE Mobile, BlackBerry
License	MIT
Programming model	Clean, familiar (jQuery-like), chaining syntax; plug-ins support
Wrapped or polyfilled HTML5 APIs	None

100% JavaScript Driven

If you prefer to create your user interface programmatically, without touching much markup, then the 100% JavaScript-driven approach may be your best option. Out of this approach, Sencha Touch, Wink Toolkit, and The-M-Project are three of the top projects.

Sencha Touch

An HTML/CSS3/JavaScript framework, Sencha Touch (*http://www.sencha.com/prod ucts/touch*) offers a variety of native-style widgets, flexible theming via SASS/Compass, data-feature-like models, stores, and proxies. Enhanced touch events and a strong data model give this framework a bit of an enterprise edge without a ton of coverage across devices (see Table 3-4). Although not in a github repository, Sencha Touch currently has around 800 followers on Twitter. (See the Sencha Touch demo (*http:// dev.sencha.com/deploy/touch/examples/production/kitchensink*).)

If you choose Sencha Touch, be aware it is a specific way of life for mobile developers. Much like GWT or JSF, you are tied to a specific development model for creating user interfaces. In jQTouch or jQuery Mobile, you write specially structured HTML. When it loads, the library reconfigures the page and turns your regular links into AJAX-based animated ones. With Sencha, you basically don't write HTML at all, but instead, you build your UI and app with JavaScript, so be prepared for a learning curve.

Table 3-4. Sencha Touch

Platform support	Android, iOS, and BlackBerry (from Sencha 1.1)
License	GPLv3, Limited Touch Commercial License
Programming model	Very little HTML; relies on writing, subclassing, and instantiating JavaScript objects

For your page setup, use the code:

```
<!DOCTYPE html>
<html>
<head>
    <meta http-equiv="Content-Type" content="text/html; charset=utf-8">
    <meta name="viewport" content="width=device-width; initial-scale=1.0;
maximum-scale=1.0; minimum-scale=1.0; user-scalable=0;" />
    <link rel="stylesheet" href="/sencha-touch.css" type="text/css">
    <title>List</title>
    <script type="text/javascript" src="/sencha-touch.js"></script>
</head>
<body></body>
</html>
```

JavaScript handles setup of your component, as well as the entire app (Figure 3-19):

```
Ext.setup({
    tabletStartupScreen: 'tablet_startup.png',
    phoneStartupScreen: 'phone_startup.png',
    icon: 'icon.png',
    glossOnIcon: false,
    onReady : function() {
        Ext.regModel('Contact', {
            fields: ['firstName', 'lastName']
        });

        var groupingBase = {
            itemTpl: '<div class="contact2"><strong>{firstName}</strong>
{lastName}</div>',
            selModel: {
                mode: 'SINGLE',
                allowDeselect: true
            },
            grouped: true,
            indexBar: false,

            onItemDisclosure: {
                scope: 'test',
                handler: function(record, btn, index) {
                    alert('Disclose more info for ' +
                                record.get('firstName'));
                }
            },

            store: new Ext.data.Store({
                model: 'Contact',
                sorters: 'firstName',

                getGroupString : function(record) {
                    return record.get('firstName')[0];
```

```
        },

        data: [
            {firstName: 'Hello', lastName: 'World'},
        ]
    })
};


if (!Ext.is.Phone) {
    new Ext.List(Ext.apply(groupingBase, {
        floating: true,
        width: 350,
        height: 370,
        centered: true,
        modal: true,
        hideOnMaskTap: false
    })).show();
}
else {
    new Ext.List(Ext.apply(groupingBase, {
        fullscreen: true
    }));
}
}
})
```

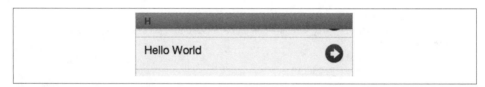

Figure 3-19. Sencha Touch List component

Wink Toolkit

The Wink Toolkit project (*http://www.winktoolkit.org*) started in early 2009 at Orange Labs (France Telecom R&D). Since June 2010, Wink has been a project of the Dojo foundation. Wink's core offers all the basic functionalities a mobile developer would need from touch event handling to DOM manipulation objects and CSS transforms utilities (Table 3-5). Additionally, it offers a wide range of UI components. Currently, its online following is low, as evidenced in Figure 3-20. (See their demo (*http://www.wink toolkit.org/wink*)).

Figure 3-20. Wink github stats, June 2012

The coolest thing about Wink is their vast set of 2D and 3D components, and the ability to manipulate components with gestures. For example, with Wink's Cover Flow component, the user can use two fingers to alter the perspective (Figure 3-21).

Figure 3-21. Wink Cover Flow 3D component

Table 3-5. Wink Toolkit

Platform support	iOS, Android, BlackBerry, and Bada
License	Simplified BSD License
Programming model	JavaScript helpers to add standard mobile browser support; UI is created inside of JavaScript snippets
Wrapped or polyfilled HTML5 APIs	Accelerometer, Geolocation, Web Storage

The HTML for page setup is:

```
<html>
    <head>
        <link rel="stylesheet" href="wink.css" type="text/css" >
        <link rel="stylesheet" href="wink.default.css" type="text/css" >
```

```
    ...
    <script type="text/javascript" src="wink.min.js"></script>
    ...
</head>
<body onload="init()">
<div class="w_box w_header w_bg_dark">
    <span id="title">accordion</span>
    <input type="button" value="home"
    class="w_button w_radius w_bg_light w_right"
  onclick="window.location='..?theme='+theme"/>
</div>

<div class="w_bloc">
    click on the accordion section below to display the content.
</div>

<div id="output" style="width: 95%; margin: auto">
</div>
</body>
</html>
```

To set up the component shown in Figure 3-22, use:

```
var accordion, section1,
section2, section3;

init = function()
{
    accordion = new wink.ui.layout.Accordion();

    section1 = accordion.addSection('Section1', 'Hello World');
    section2 = accordion.addSection('section2', '...');
    section3 = accordion.addSection('section3', '...');

    $('output').appendChild(accordion.getDomNode());
}

deleteSection = function()
{
    accordion.deleteSection(section2);
```

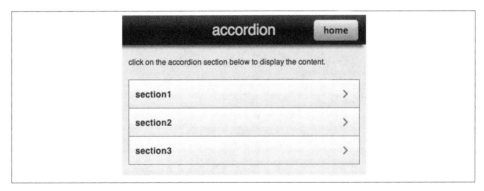

Figure 3-22. Wink Accordion component

The-M-Project

The-M-Project (*http://the-m-project.net*) (their demo (*http://www.the-m-project.org/apps/kitchensink*)) is built on top of jQuery and jQuery Mobile. It uses concepts and parts from SproutCore and bases its persistence handling on *persistence.js*. Figure 3-23 gives a snapshot of its community following.

Figure 3-23. The-M-Project github stats; June 2012

Because The-M-Project UI looks exactly like jQuery Mobile, it's hard to tell at first glance what the big difference is. The project, however, is much more than a shiny UI framework. It has four core development concepts: MVC, Content Binding, Dynamic Value Computing, and Event Handling. So unlike the UI-focused Wink Toolkit, The-M-Project puts most of its focus on the programming model, as you can see in Table 3-6.

Table 3-6. The-M-Project

Platform support	iOS, Android, WebOS, BlackBerry, Windows Phone
License	GPLv2 and MIT
Programming model	Relies heavily on MVC pattern; creates view components through JavaScript and addresses data binding
Wrapped or polyfilled HTML5 APIs	Web Storage (DataProvider for local and remote storage persistence)

A bit of JavaScript handles page setup:

```
PageSwitchDemo.Page1 =
M.PageView.design({
    childViews: 'header content',
    header: M.ToolbarView.design({
        value: 'Page 1'
```

```
        }),
        content: M.ScrollView.design({
            childViews: 'button',
            button: M.ButtonView.design({
                value: 'Goto Page 2',
                events: {
                    tap: {
                        target: PageSwitchDemo.ApplicationController,
                        action: 'gotoPage2'
                    }
                }
            })
        })

    });
```

To create the component shown in Figure 3-24, use:

```
M.SelectionListView.design({

    childViews: 'item1 item2 item3 item4',
    /* renders a selection view like radio buttons */
    selectionMode: M.SINGLE_SELECTION,

    item1: M.SelectionListItemView.design({
        value: 'item1',
        label: 'Item 1',
        isSelected: YES
    }),
    item2: M.SelectionListItemView.design({
        value: 'item2',
        label: 'Item 2'
    }),
    item3: M.SelectionListItemView.design({
        value: 'item3',
        label: 'Item 3'
    }),
    item4: M.SelectionListItemView.design
        value: 'item4',
        label: 'Item 4'
    })
});
```

Figure 3-24. The-M-Project List component

Of course, many other frameworks—SproutCore, Jo, Zepto, LungoJS, the list goes on—are available. All of these frameworks contain useful features and building blocks for everyday programming of mobile web apps. Some even try to create a wrapper or proxy for spec-driven features like Web Storage. But, it seems they all have a gaping hole in terms of the needs of enterprise developers and a consistent architecture across device browsers.

Mobile Debugging

In the world of desktop-based web development, we have many tools at our disposal for debugging. Firebug and Chrome's developer tools are a few that help us get the job done faster. For mobile, the situation is much different, and we must remotely debug through third-party tools. Luckily, projects like weinre, Adobe Shadow, and Opera's Remote Debugging tools try to give developers the same debugging experience as desktop environments.

weinre

Like FireBug for FireFox and Web Inspector for WebKit-based browsers, weinre (*http:// people.apache.org/~pmuellr/weinre*) is a debugger for web pages. Its difference is that it is designed to work remotely and, in particular, to allow you debug web pages on a mobile device, such as a phone. If you've used Safari's Web Inspector or Chrome's Developer Tools, weinre will be very familiar (Figure 3-25).

Figure 3-25. A demo of weinre in action

For debug clients, weinre supports:

- weinre Mac application (Mac OS X 10.6 64-bit)
- Google Chrome 8.x
- Apple Safari 5.x

For debug targets, weinre supports:

- Android 2.2 Browser application
- Android 2.2 with PhoneGap 0.9.2
- iOS 4.2.x Mobile Safari application
- BlackBerry v6.x simulator
- webOS 2.x (unspecified version)

Adobe Shadow

Shown in Figure 3-26, Adobe Shadow (*http://labs.adobe.com/technologies/shadow*) is an inspection and preview tool that streamlines the preview process for Android and iOS mobile devices. After installing Shadow on your computer, you'll be able to wirelessly pair your devices, have them browse in sync with your computer, and perform remote inspection and debugging so you can see HTML/CSS/JavaScript changes instantly on your device. Some of Shadow's features include the ability to:

- Wirelessly pair your iOS devices to your computer
- Synchronously browse with your computer
- Target a device for debugging and select an element in the DOM
- Make changes to your HTML markup
- Tweak your CSS rules
- See changes instantly on your device

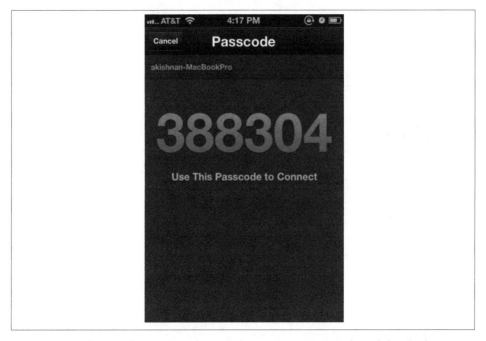

Figure 3-26. The autodiscovery and passcode connection screen for Adobe Shadow

Opera Remote Debugging

Using the remote debugging functionality of Opera Dragonfly (*http://www.opera.com/dragonfly/documentation/remote*), you can analyze and debug pages running in the Opera Mobile Emulator (see Figure 3-27). With Dragonfly, you can debug in separate instances of the Opera browser, as well as other Opera Presto-powered user agents. It doesn't matter if these are located on the same machine or on another device such as a mobile phone or television. When put into Remote Debugging mode, Opera Dragonfly will listen for a connection to the IP address and port specified. The separate instance of the Opera browser can connect over a network and pass debugging information across the connection. Opera Dragonfly can then interact with the web pages and applications on the remote instance, just as if it were running locally.

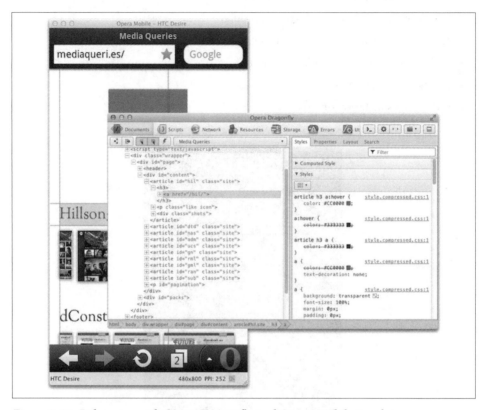

Figure 3-27. Debugging with Opera Dragonfly and Opera Mobile Emulator

## CHAPTER 4

The Desktop Web

The rest of this book covers support and features for all browsers, both desktop and mobile. In the first three chapters, we talked about mobile browsers and what it takes to build a mobile web app. For the desktop, things are getting better in terms of supporting HTML5 and what this book defines as HTML5e. Comparing Table 4-1 to Table 2-2 in Chapter 2, you can see that support for the five core frameworks is exactly the same, if not better, in desktop browsers. Because of this, we can feel comfortable bringing HTML5 into our production applications today.

Table 4-1. HTML5 Enterprise (HTML5e)

Browser	Geolocation	WebSocket	Web Storage	Device Orientation	Web Workers
Safari 5+	Yes	Yes	Yes	Unknown	Yes
Chrome 19+	Yes	Yes	Yes	Yes	Yes
IE 10+	Yes	Yes	Yes	Unknown	Yes
Opera 12+	Yes	Yes	Yes	No	Yes
Firefox 12+	Yes	Yes	Yes	Yes	Yes

Of course, you will notice some differences in support. For example, Device Orientation may not make a lot of sense for desktop browsers, but it is supported in Chrome and Firefox browsers.

 Although Geolocation does not fall under HTML5, I am including it under HTML5e because of its value to modern web apps and its wide support in most browsers.

The Browser as a Platform

To some, server-side UI frameworks, which automatically generate JavaScript, CSS, and HTML, are the saviors of enterprise development. To others, those UI frameworks create a massive bottleneck and tie you to stale ideas and structures.

Today, developers are forced to look at web application architecture from a different perspective where the browser and JavaScript are taking just as much spotlight as server-side code (or in some cases, JavaScript is the server-side code).

Client Versus Server HTML Generation

Somewhere between 2008 and 2009, the server-heavy culture of generating HTML and other resources on the backend broke down. This was mostly due to the progressive enhancement of web pages with AJAX and other performance optimizations. This way of thinking forced developers to create better APIs and more efficient ways of delivering data to web applications through JSON and XML.

Generating HTML on the client reduces server load and can deliver a better overall user experience. JSON and XML use less bandwidth than presentation-ready HTML, and there is less string concatenation and HTML escaping to perform. The client browser must download the first payload of JavaScript and markup, but after that, it's much easier to control how resources are delivered and how the application is enhanced. This also gives you the flexibility of using CDN bandwidth for such popular libraries as jQuery. When using a CDN for resource delivery, you are betting that the user has already downloaded this library through another website using the same CDN. This spares users the bulk and expense of downloading a 33K (gzipped) library like jQuery yet again.

When everything runs on the client, however, performance is reduced. Parsing JSON or XML and generating HTML uses more memory and processing time than just printing some server-rendered HTML.

Whether you are generating HTML on the client or the server, there are pros and cons to each approach.

The client-side approach offers these benefits:

- Better user experience
- Network bandwidth reduction (decreases cost)
- Portability (offline capable)

The most notable client-side con is security. When you create an offline-capable application that is distributed across many different browsers, WebStorage (`localStorage`) is the only viable means for storing data on the client—and it offers no security.

The pluses to using the server-side approach are:

- Better security
- Reduces processing expense on client (battery life on mobile, and so on)
- Expandability (adding more servers can increase load capability)

Server-side rendering has its advantages, and if you are creating a web application that must be connected to the Internet at all times, then you might consider a framework that falls into this realm. When choosing a server-side framework, however, be sure that all markup is easily changeable and editable. You don't want to be stuck with a prebuilt component that is automatically generated and does not allow you to pass through newer HTML5 attributes and tags.

Overall, the main goal between generating markup on the server or the client should be to avoid ending up with a huge mess. Most of the time, you'll end up with a hybrid application that does some processing on the server and much more on the client. So you want to be sure that the code is properly distributed and organized. Dealing with two separate code bases that interact with each other takes special care. Using a client side MV* framework (like Backbone or Knockout) forces a clean separation of concerns when querying server APIs for data. (You'll learn more about this topic later in the chapter.)

In regard to recent applications that have taken the step toward more client-side processing, LinkedIn launched its new HTML5-based mobile web app in late 2011 (Figure 4-1). The company's mobile development lead gave the following statement in an interview (*http://venturebeat.com/2011/08/16/linkedin-node*):

> The app is 2 to 10 times faster on the client side than its predecessor, and on the server side, it's using a fraction of the resources, thanks to a switch from Ruby on Rails to *Node.js*, a server-side JavaScript development technology that's barely a year old but already rapidly gaining traction.

With heavily used applications like LinkedIn's mobile HTML5 web app turning to newer technologies such as *Node.js* and JavaScript-heavy client-side code, we can see the world of web application development evolving and changing. This world is ever-changing and will continue to change as years go by, but how do we build a performant client-side solution in today's new world of client- and server-side technologies? Your answer is at hand. This chapter reviews everything it takes to set up the appropriate HTML5 infrastructure for your web app. Certain APIs, such as WebSockets and Web Storage, will be given more emphasis and examples in subsequent chapters. Think of this chapter as a setup script for the rest of the book.

Figure 4-1. LinkedIn Mobile Web

Device and Feature Detection

The first step in delivering new HTML5-based features to your user base is actually detecting what the browser supports. You need to communicate with the browser to see what it supports before the page is even rendered. In the past, you were forced to detect and parse the—sometimes unreliable—browser userAgent (UA) string and then assume you had the correct device. Today, such frameworks as *Modernizr.js* or just simple Java-Script, help you detect client-side capabilities at a much more finely grained level.

Which detection method is best? The feature-detection approach is new, but growing, while the approach of parsing the userAgent string is flawed and should be handled with caution. Even at the time of this writing, browser vendors are still getting it wrong. The userAgent string for the latest phone-based Firefox on Android, for example, reports itself as a tablet not a phone. Mozilla uses the exact same userAgent string for both phones and tablets, and that string has the word "Android" in both. The key to success is understanding how you can use each approach most effectively, either by itself or to complement the other.

Client-Side Feature Detection

JavaScript-based feature detection is often implemented by creating a DOM element to see if it exists or behaves as expected, for example:

```
detectCanvas() ? showGraph() :
showTable();

function detectCanvas() {
  var canvas = document.createElement("canvas");
  return canvas.getContext ? true : false;
}
```

This snippet creates a canvas element and checks to see if it supports the `getContext` property. Checking a property of the created element is a must, because browsers will allow you to create any element in the DOM, whether it's supported or not.

This approach is one of many, and today we have open source, community-backed frameworks that do the heavy lifting for us. Here's the same code as above, implemented with the Modernizr framework:

```
Modernizr.canvas ? showGraph()
: showTable();
```

Feature-detection frameworks may come at a cost, however. Suppose you are running a series of tests on the browser window before the page is rendered. This can get expensive: running the full suite of Modernizr detections, for example, can take more than 30 milliseconds to run per page load. You must consider the costs of computing values before DOM render and then modifying the DOM based on the framework's findings. When you're ready to take your app to production, make sure you're not using the development version of your chosen feature detection library.

On the plus side, frameworks like Modernizr provide a build tool that enables you to pick and choose the features your app must have (Figure 4-2). You can select exactly which features you want to detect, and thereby reduce the overall detection footprint in a production environment.

Feature-detection performance also depends on the devices and browsers you are targeting. For example, running a feature-detection framework on a first-generation smartphone or old BlackBerry could crash the browser and cause your app to fail completely. Take the time to tweak feature detection to gain top performance on your target browsers.

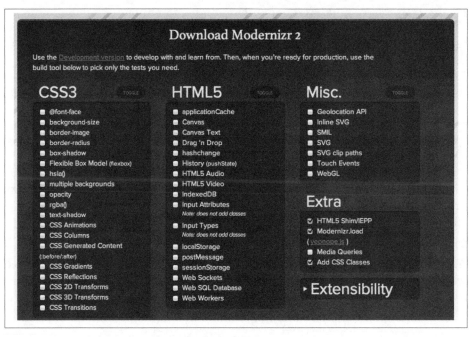

Figure 4-2. Modernizr production configuration choices

Sometimes, as well, you may need to go a step further and detect the actual form factor of the device. *FormFactor.js* can help you with this. It helps you customize your web app for different form factors (a mobile version, a TV version, and the like). For example:

```
if(formfactor.is("tv")) {
  alert("Look ma, Im on tv!");
}

if(formfactor.isnt("tv")) {
  alert("The revolution will not be televised");
}
```

Because *FormFactor.js* is a framework to manage conceptually distinct user interfaces, it doesn't eliminate the need for feature detection. It does, however, help you to use feature detection in the context of a particular form factor's interface.

Although the community has gone a bit inactive lately, you can find more examples at *https://github.com/PaulKinlan/formfactor*.

Client-Side userAgent Detection

There are times when you must detect the userAgent and parse it accordingly. Typically, you can determine the browser by inspecting JavaScript's window.navigator object or by using the userAgent request header on the server side. This approach may work for most browsers, but it's not dependable, as noted in a recent bug report for the MobileESP project:

> Issue Summary: When using the Firefox browser on an Android mobile phone, the MobileESP code library erroneously reports the device as an Android tablet. An Android tablet is correctly identified as an Android tablet. This issue only affects mobile phones and similar small-screen Android devices like MP3 players (such as the Samsung Galaxy Player).

> Root Cause: Mozilla uses the exact same userAgent string for both phones and tablets. The string has the word 'Android' in both. According to Google guidelines, Mozilla should include the word 'mobile' in the userAgent string for mobile phones. Unfortunately, Mozilla is not compliant with Google's guidelines. The omission of the word 'mobile' is the reason why phones are erroneously identified as tablets.

So if userAgent detection isn't always dependable, when is it a good choice to use?

- When you know, ahead of time, which platforms you are supporting and their UA strings report correctly. For example, if you care about only the environment (not its features) your application is running in, such as iOS, you could deliver a custom UI for that environment only.

- When you use it in combination with feature-detection JavaScript that calls only the minimum functions needed to check the device. For example, you may not care about the discrepancy in the reported string, because it's unneeded information. You might only care that it reports TV, and everything else is irrelevant. This also allows for "light" feature detection via JavaScript.

- When you don't want all JavaScript-based feature tests to be downloaded to every browser and executed when optimizations based on userAgent-sniffing are available.

Yahoo! has its own reasons for using userAgent detection:

> At Yahoo we have a database full of around 10,000 mobile devices. Because userAgent strings vary even on one device (because of locale, vendor, versioning, etc.), this has resulted in well over a half a *million* user agents. It's become pretty crazy to maintain, but is necessary because there's really no alternative for all these feature phones, which can't even run JavaScript.

On the other hand, Google and other companies opt for a JavaScript-based (also ported to *node.js*) userAgent parser internally. It's a wrapper for an approximately 7Kb JSON file, which can be used in other languages. You can find more information at *https://github.com/Tobie/Ua-parser*, but here is a snippet:

```
var uaParser =
require('ua-parser');
var ua = uaParser.parse(navigator.userAgent);

console.log(ua.tostring());
// -> "Safari 5.0.1"

console.log(ua.toVersionString());
// -> "5.0.1"

console.log(ua.toFullString());
// -> "Safari 5.0.1/Mac OS X"

console.log(ua.family);
// -> "Safari"

console.log(ua.major);
// -> 5

console.log(ua.minor);
// -> 0

console.log(ua.patch);
// -> 1

console.log(ua.os);
// -> Mac OS X
```

Another platform detection library written in JavaScript is *Platform.js*. It's used by jsperf.com for userAgent detection. *Platform.js* has been tested in at least Adobe AIR 2.6, Chrome 5–15, Firefox 1.5–8, IE 6–10, Opera 9.25–11.52, Safari 2–5.1.1, *Node.js* 0.4.8–0.6.1, Narwhal 0.3.2, RingoJS 0.7–0.8, and Rhino 1.7RC3. (For more information, see *https://github.com/Bestiejs/Platform.js*.)

The following example shows the results returned from various browsers when using *Platform.js*:

```
// on IE10 x86 platform
preview running in IE7 compatibility mode on
// Windows 7 64 bit edition
platform.name; // 'IE'
platform.version; // '10.0'
platform.layout; // 'Trident'
platform.os; // 'Windows Server 2008 R2 / 7 x64'
platform.description; // 'IE 10.0 x86 (platform preview; running in IE 7 mode) on Windows
Server 2008 R2 / 7 x64'
```

```
// or on an iPad
platform.name; // 'Safari'
platform.version; // '5.1'
platform.product; // 'iPad'
platform.manufacturer; // 'Apple'
platform.layout; // 'WebKit'
platform.os; // 'iOS 5.0'
platform.description; // 'Safari 5.1 on Apple iPad (iOS 5.0)'

// or parsing a given UA string
var info = platform.parse('Mozilla/5.0 (Macintosh;
                           Intel Mac OS X 10.7.2; en; rv:2.0)
Gecko/20100101 Firefox/4.0 Opera 11.52');
info.name; // 'Opera'
info.version; // '11.52'
info.layout; // 'Presto'
info.os; // 'Mac OS X 10.7.2'
info.description; // 'Opera 11.52 (identifying as Firefox 4.0) on Mac OS X
10.7.2'
```

Server-Side userAgent Detection

On the server side, MobileESP (*http://blog.mobileesp.com*) is an open source framework, which detects the userAgent header. This gives you the ability to direct the user to the appropriate page and allows other developers to code to supported device features.

MobileESP is available in six languages:

- PHP
- Java (server side)
- ASP.NET (C#)
- JavaScript
- Ruby
- Classic ASP (VBscript)

In Java, you would use:

```
userAgentStr =
request.getHeader("user-agent");
httpAccept = request.getHeader("Accept");
uAgentTest = new UAgentInfo(userAgentStr, httpAccept);

If(uAgentTest.detectTierIphone()){
...//Perform redirect
}
```

In PHP, the code would be:

```php
<?php

        //Load the Mobile Detection library
        include("code/mdetect.php");

        //In this simple example, we'll store the alternate home page
        // file names.
        $iphoneTierHomePage = 'index-tier-iphone.htm';

        //Instantiate the object to do our testing with.
        $uagent_obj = new uagent_info();

        //In this simple example, we simply re-route depending on
        // which type of device it is.
        //Before we can call the function, we have to define it.
        function AutoRedirectToProperHomePage()
        {
            global $uagent_obj, $iphoneTierHomePage,
                $genericMobileDeviceHomePage, $desktopHomePage;

            if ($uagent_obj->isTierIphone == $uagent_obj->true)
            //Perform redirect
        }
```

So there you have it, userAgent detection is unreliable and should be used with caution or for specific cases only. Even in the scenario described by the Android/Firefox bug report, for example, you could still implement userAgent detection and then use feature detection to find the maximum screen size for Android-based mobile phones using CSS Media Queries. There's always a workaround, and problems such as these should not deter you from using the userAgent string.

Compression

Compression of resources is mandatory in today's mobile-first priority. If you aren't concerned with the size of your HTML, JavaScript, and CSS files, you should be. HTTP compression is used to achieve a minimal transfer of bytes over a given web-based connection. This reduces response times by reducing the size of the HTTP response. The two commonly used HTTP compression schemes on the Web today are DEFLATE and GZIP (more on these coming up).

When you gain performance on the client side, however, it's easy to forget about increased overhead on your server resources. If you have complex SQL queries that increase the CPU load to present certain pages, you should analyze the effects of using HTTP compression when these scenarios occur. Compressing a huge page that surpasses 20 to 30K may have a negative effect on your application's performance. In this case, the expense of compressing the data will be completely dwarfed by the expense of the SQL work on the server side. A few other considerations to take into account before flipping the compression switch on every request are:

- Ensure you are compressing only compressible content and not wasting resources trying to compress uncompressible content
- Select the correct compression scheme for your visitors
- Configure the web server properly so compressed content is sent to capable clients

So, what should be compressed? Along with the obvious resources such as HTML, Java-Script, and CSS, several common text resource types should be served with HTTP compression:

- XML.
- JSON.
- News feeds (both RSS and Atom feeds are XML documents).
- HTML Components (HTC). HTC files are a proprietary Internet Explorer feature that package markup, style, and code information used for CSS behaviors. HTC files are often used by polyfills (*https://github.com/Modernizr/Modernizr/wiki/HTML5-Cross-Browser-Polyfills*), such as Pie (*http://css3pie.com/*) or *iepngfix.htc* (*http://www.twinhelix.com/css/iepngfix/*), to fix various problems with IE or to back port modern functionality.
- Plain text files can come in many forms, from README and LICENSE files, to Markdown (*http://en.wikipedia.org/wiki/Markdown*) files. All should be compressed.
- A text file used to tell search engines what parts of the website to crawl, *Robots.txt* often forgotten, because it is not usually accessed by humans. Because *robots.txt* is repeatedly accessed by search engine crawlers and can be quite large, it can consume large amounts of bandwidth without your knowledge.
- Anything that isn't natively compressed should be allowed through HTTP compression. HTTP compression isn't just for text resources and should be applied to all nonnatively compressed file formats. For example, Favicons (ICO), SVG, and BMP image files are not natively compressed. ICO files are served up as an icon for your site in the URL bar or tab of most browsers, so be sure these filed receive HTTP compression.

GZIP Versus DEFLATE

The top two HTTP compression schemes are by far GZIP and DEFLATE. GZIP was developed by the GNU project and standardized by RFC 1952 (*http://www.ietf.org/rfc/rfc1952.txt*). GZIP is the most popular compression method currently available and generally reduces the response size by about 70%. DEFLATE is a patent-free compression algorithm for lossless data compression. There are numerous open source implementations of the algorithm. Apache's mod_deflate module is one implementation that many developers are familiar with.

 To learn more about the differences between GZIP and DEFLATE compression, see Billy Hoffman's excellent article at *http://zoompf.com/2012/02/lose-the-wait-http-compression*.

Approximately 90% of today's Internet traffic travels through browsers that claim to support GZIP. All browsers supporting DEFLATE also support GZIP, but all browsers that support GZIP do not support DEFLATE. Some browsers, such as Android, don't include DEFLATE in their Accept-Encoding request header. Because you are going to have to configure your web server to use GZIP anyway, you might as well avoid the whole mess with Content-Encoding: deflate.

The Apache module that handles all HTTP compression is mod_deflate. Despite its name, mod_deflate doesn't support DEFLATE at all. It's impossible to get a stock version of Apache 2 to send either raw DEFLATE or zlib-wrapped DEFLATE. Nginx (*http://nginx.org/*), like Apache, does not support DEFLATE at all and sends only GZIP-compressed responses. Sending an Accept-Encoding: deflate request header will result in an uncompressed response.

If you use Apache, the module configuring GZIP depends on your version: Apache 1.3 uses mod_gzip (*http://sourceforge.net/projects/mod-gzip/*), while Apache 2.x uses mod_deflate (*http://httpd.apache.org/docs/2.0/mod/mod_deflate.html*). Again, despite the naming convention, both use GZIP under the hood.

The following is a simple example of how to match certain file types to include in HTTP compression. You would place it in the *.htaccess* file in Apache 2.4:

```
AddOutputFilterByType DEFLATE text/html text/plain
text/xml
```

Here's a more complex example that deals with browser inconsistencies can be set as follows to compress everything except images:

```
<Location
/>
# Insert filter
SetOutputFilter DEFLATE
```

```
# Netscape 4.x has some problems...
BrowserMatch ^Mozilla/4        gzip-only-text/html

# Netscape 4.06-4.08 have some more problems
BrowserMatch ^Mozilla/4\.0[678] no-gzip

# MSIE masquerades as Netscape, but it is fine
BrowserMatch \bMSIE            !no-gzip
!gzip-only-text/html

# Don't compress images
SetEnvIfNoCase Request_URI \.(?:gif|jpe?g|png)$ no-gzip
dont-vary

# Make sure proxies don't deliver the wrong content
Header append Vary User-Agent env=!dont-vary
</Location>
```

The community project HTML5Boilerplate.com (*http://html5boilerplate.com*) contains an excellent example of an optimized *.htaccess* file. It's specifically crafted for web performance optimizations. It provides a great starting point for implementing HTTP compression properly. It also serves as a nice guide to compare to an existing web server configuration to verify you are following best practices (*https://github.com/h5bp/html5-boilerplate/blob/master/.htaccess*).

You can view most other major server configurations for HTTP compression in the github repository for HTML5Boilerplate (*https://github.com/h5bp/server-configs*), as well as Figure 4-3. Some of the configurations included are:

- Node.js
- IIS
- Nginx
- lighttpd
- Google App Engine

After you think you have properly configured your web server from a compression and optimization point of view, you must validate it. Web Sniffer (*http://web-sniffer.net/*) is an excellent, free, web-based tool that enables you make individual HTTP requests and see the responses. As you can see in Figure 4-4, Web Sniffer gives you some control over the userAgent and Accept-Encoding headers to ensure that compressed content is delivered properly.

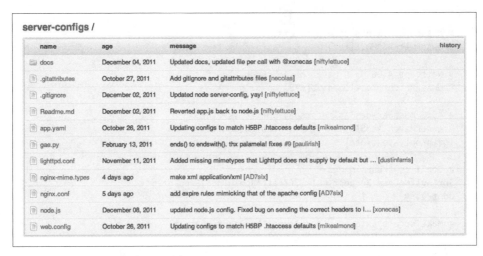

Figure 4-3. H5BP github examples

For more information on HTTP see **RFC 2616**

HTTP(S)-URL: [   ] [Submit]
(IDN allowed)

HTTP version: ⦿ HTTP/1.1 ◯ HTTP/1.0 (with Host header) ◯
HTTP/1.0 (without Host header)

◻ Raw HTML view ☑ Accept-Encoding: gzip • Request type: ⦿ GET
◯ POST ◯ HEAD ◯ TRACE

User agent: [Web-Sniffer   ⇕]

[ⓕ Flattr] [121]

Features:

- list of user agents
- switch between HTTP/1.1 and HTTP/1.0
- test If-Modified-Since and If-Match headers
- support WWW-Authenticate
- search engine redirect added – all bots will be moved permanently
  to frontpage
- the URL may also be an Internationalized Domain Names (IDN)
- secure connections (HTTPS) allowed

Figure 4-4. Customize HTTP request and response headers with Web Sniffer

Minification

The need for JavaScript and CSS compression to keep bandwidth and page load times as small as possible is becoming more important to ensuring faster load times and more enjoyable user experiences. *Minification* is the process of removing all unnecessary characters from source code, without changing its functionality.

JavaScript and CSS resources may be minified, preserving their behavior while considerably reducing their file size. Some libraries also merge multiple script files into a single file for client download. This fosters a modular approach to development and limits HTTP requests.

Google has released its Closure Compiler tool, which provides minification as well as the ability to introduce more aggressive renaming. It also can remove dead code and provide function inlining. In addition, certain online tools, such as Microsoft Ajax Minifier, the Yahoo! YUI Compressor, and Pretty Diff, can compress CSS files. Some of your choices are:

JSMin (http://www.crockford.com/javascript/jsmin.html)
> JSMin is a conservative compressor, written several years ago by Douglas Crockford. It is a filter that removes comments and unnecessary whitespace from JavaScript files. It typically reduces file size by half, resulting in faster downloads. It also encourages a more expressive programming style, because it eliminates the download cost of clean, literate self-documentation. It's recommended you use JSLint before minimizing your JavaScript with JSMin.

Packer (http://dean.edwards.name/packer)
> Packer, by Dean Edwards, is also a very popular JavaScript compressor, which can go beyond regular compression and also add advanced on-the-fly decompression with a JavaScript runtime piece. For example, Packer can optionally base64 compress the given source code in a manner that can be decompressed by regular web browsers, as well as shrink variable names that are typically 5 to 10 characters to single letters, which reduces the file size of the script and, therefore, makes it download faster.

Dojo ShrinkSafe (http://dojotoolkit.org/docs/shrinksafe)
> Dojo ShrinkSafe is a very popular Java-based JavaScript compressor that parses the JavaScript using the Rhino (*http://www.mozilla.org/rhino/*) library and crunches local variable names.

YUI Compressor (http://developer.yahoo.com/yui/compressor/)
> The YUI Compressor is a newer compressor written by Julien Lecomte that aims to combine the safety of JSMin with the higher compression levels achieved by Dojo ShrinkSafe. Like Dojo ShrinkSafe, it is written in Java and based on the Rhino (*http://www.mozilla.org/rhino/*) library.

How do you choose a minifier? CompressorRater (*http://compressorrater.thruhere.net/*) can help. CompressorRater is a tool to rate and evaluate all of the aforementioned minification tools at one time (Figure 4-5).

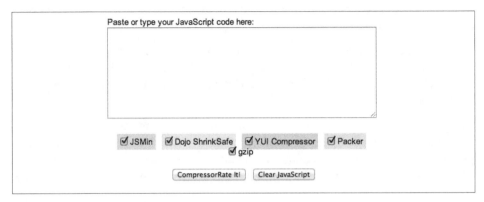

Figure 4-5. CompressorRater

Bringing it all together

As you've seen, there are many tools and options to choose from when minifying and concatenating your code. Fortunately, there has been a recent community effort to bring all of these projects together into one common build tool: it's called grunt.

More than a simple minifier, grunt (*https://github.com/cowboy/grunt*) is a task-based command-line build tool for frontend projects. With it, you can concatenate files, validate files with JSHint, and minify with UglifyJS. In addition, grunt enables your project to run headless QUnit tests with a PhantomJS instance.

grunt is available as an npm (node-packaged module), which is the nodejs way of managing installable packages (*http://npmjs.org*). If you install grunt globally with:

```
npm install -g grunt
```

it will be available for use in all of your projects. Once grunt has been installed, you can type **grunt --help** at the command line for more information. Then, your available tasks are:

concat
    Concatenate files

init
    Generate project scaffolding from a predefined template

lint
    Validate files with JSHint

min

Minify files with UglifyJS

qunit

Run QUnit unit tests in a headless PhantomJS instance

server

Start a static web server

test

Run unit tests with nodeunit)

watch

Run predefined tasks whenever watched files change

The following code is an example of a very basic sample *grunt.js* file that handles project configuration, loading a grunt plug-in, and a default task:

```
module.exports =
function(grunt) {
  // Project configuration.
  grunt.initConfig({
    lint: {
      all: ['grunt.js', 'lib/**/*.js''test/**/*.js']
    },
    jshint: {
      options: {
        browser: true
      }
    }
  });

  // Load tasks from "grunt-sample" grunt plugin installed via Npm.
  grunt.loadNpmTasks('grunt-sample');

  // Default task.
  grunt.registerTask('default', 'lint sample');

};
```

You can easily set up a new grunt project by using the grunt `init` command. There are a few different templates for various types of projects including CommonJS, jQuery, and Node.js.

As an example, try running grunt on the *slidfast.js* library used in the previous chapters. From the root of the project, in the terminal, run:

```
grunt init:gruntfile
```

This customizable template (Figure 4-6) creates a single *grunt.js* file based on your answers to a few questions. Grunt also tries to determine source, unit test, and other system paths using it's own environment detection.

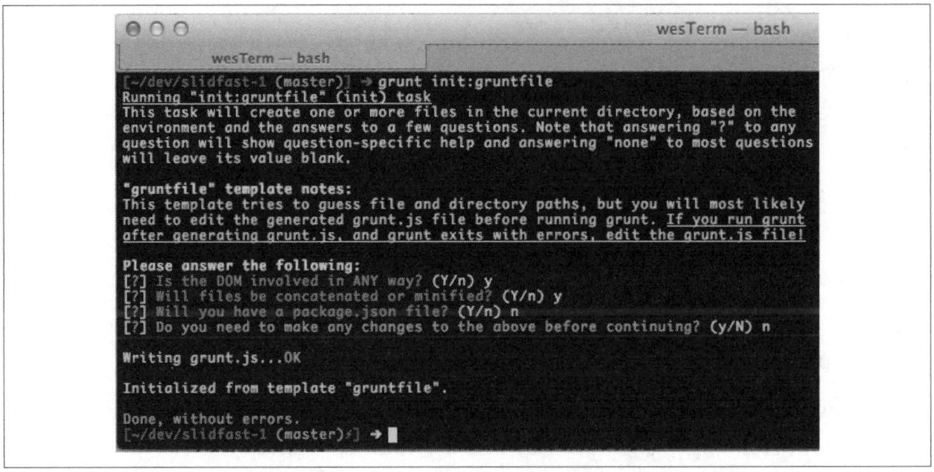

Figure 4-6. Running grunt init:gruntfile from Terminal

Each time grunt runs, it looks in the current directory for a file named *grunt.js*. If this file is not found, grunt continues looking in parent directories until that file is found. This file is typically placed in the root of your project repository, and is a valid JavaScript file composed of three parts:

- Project configuration
- Loading grunt plug-ins or tasks folders
- Tasks and helpers

This is what the *grunt.js* looks like for the *slidfast.js* (*https://github.com/html5e/slidfast*) JavaScript project (which only includes HTML, CSS, and JavaScript files):

```
/*global module:false*/
module.exports = function(grunt) {

  // Project configuration.
  grunt.initConfig({
    meta: {
      version: '0.1.0',
      banner: '/*! PROJECT_NAME - v<%= meta.version %> - ' +
        '<%= grunt.template.today("yyyy-mm-dd") %>\n' +
        '* http://PROJECT_WEBSITE/\n' +
        '* Copyright (c) <%= grunt.template.today("yyyy") %> ' +
        'YOUR_NAME; Licensed MIT */'
    },
    lint: {
      files: ['grunt.js', 'slidfast.js']
    },
//    qunit: {
```

```
//      files: ['example/**/*.html']
//    },
    concat: {
      dist: {
        src: ['<banner:meta.banner>', '<file_strip_banner:slidfast.js>'],
        dest: 'dist/slidfast.js'
      }
    },
    min: {
      dist: {
        src: ['<banner:meta.banner>', '<config:concat.dist.dest>'],
        dest: 'dist/slidfast.min.js'
      }
    },
    watch: {
      files: '<config:lint.files>',
      tasks: 'lint qunit'
    },
    jshint: {
      options: {
        curly: true,
        eqeqeq: true,
        immed: true,
        latedef: true,
        newcap: true,
        noarg: true,
        sub: true,
        undef: true,
        boss: true,
        eqnull: true,
        browser: true
      },
      globals: {}
    },
    uglify: {}
  });

  // Default task.
  grunt.registerTask('default', 'lint concat min');

};
```

 Because no QUnit tests are currently defined for this project, I commented out the default values and removed it from the last line in the file.

Now, if you run grunt within your project by simply typing **grunt** at the command line, grunt returns a log like the one in Figure 4-7. As you can see in the example log, grunt lists where the JavaScript lint fails. In addition, because this example bypassed the lint process by using `grunt -force`, grunt was able to continue minifying the files and display the before and after size of the files.

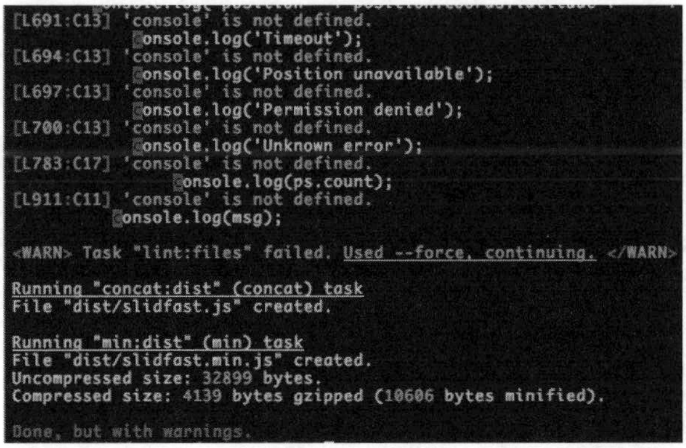

Figure 4-7. Running grunt from the command line

Two more multipurpose tools useful for minifying are Jawr and Ziproxy.

Jawr (*http://jawr.java.net*) is a tunable packaging solution for JavaScript and CSS that allows for rapid development of resources in separate module files. You can work with a large set of split JavaScript files in development mode, then Jawr bundles them all together into one or several files in a configurable way. By using a tag library, Jawr enables you to use the same, unchanged pages for development and production. Jawr also minifies and compresses the files, resulting in reduced page load times. You can configure Jawr using a simple `.properties` descriptor. Besides standard Java web applications, it can also be used with Facelets and Grails applications.

Ziproxy (*http://ziproxy.sourceforge.net*) is a forwarding, noncaching, compressing HTTP proxy targeted for traffic optimization. It minifies and optimizes HTML, CSS, and JavaScript resources, plus recompresses pictures. Basically, it squeezes images by converting them to lower quality JPEGs or JPEG 2000 and compresses (via GZIP) HTML and other text-like data. In addition, it provides such features as preemptive hostname resolution, transparent proxying, IP ToS marking (QoS), Ad-Blocker, detailed logging, and more. Ziproxy does not require client software and provides acceleration for any web browser on any OS.

JavaScript MVC Frameworks and the Server

With the myriad of JavaScript MV* (aka MVC) frameworks popping up over the past few years, it's important to get a high-level view of what frameworks are available today and how they support some form of server-side interaction.

In theory, JavaScript frameworks offer developers an easy path to organizing code. After a few years of attempting to manually organize AJAX/jQuery callbacks, the development community recognized the need to create frameworks around frontend code. Developers realized that complex client-side applications do not scale with spaghetti code and that keeping up with manually bound, AJAX-returned data using `innerHTML()` can get quite messy. So the solution was to use variations of a pattern known as *MVC* (*Model-View-Controller*). MVC separates the concerns in an application down into three parts:

- Models
- Views
- Controllers

Although JavaScript MVC frameworks help us structure our code, they don't always strictly follow the classic pattern shown in Figure 4-8. Some frameworks will include the responsibility of the controller in the view such as *Backbone.js* (*http://backbo nejs.org/*), while others add their own opinionated components into the mix, as they feel this is more effective.

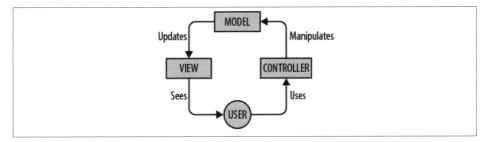

Figure 4-8. The MVC process

For this reason, I refer to such frameworks as following the MV* pattern; that is, you're likely to have a view and a model, but more likely to have something else also included. If your goal is to learn the basics of each MV* framework on the market today, TodoMVC (Figure 4-9) provides implementations of a to-do app in more frameworks than anyone has time to learn. Currently there are around 40 JavaScript MV* frameworks in existence. Choosing the right framework for a given project is the start of your journey.

Figure 4-9. TodoMVC is a collection of to-do demos built for most JavaScript MV* frameworks

The Top Five Frameworks

Before you can decide which framework is best for your project, you need to know how they perform. The following sections focus on how each of the five leading frameworks handles server-side collections of objects rendered to the DOM. Data interaction is important for two main reasons:

- Binding objects to the UI must be declarative, and the view layer should autoupdate as changes to the model occur.

- It's easy to create JavaScript-heavy applications that end up as a tangled mess of jQuery, RESTful endpoints, and callbacks. A structured MVC approach makes code more maintainable and reusable.

For each framework, I'll evaluate persistence strategies, identify JavaScript frameworks that are server agnostic, and use transports such as HTTP (for RESTful endpoints) and other protocols such as WebSockets. This section assumes you already have a basic idea of what a JavaScript MV* framework is and does. I will not go into details on how well each framework implements the original Smalltalk MVC pattern, rather the discussions focus on how each framework synchronizes data from the server to the client and vice versa.

Choosing the right framework and using it well comes down to knowing what you need. Beyond the five frameworks I review in this section, there are many others you can use in your application. Weigh out the pros and cons of each one, and find the right development model for your targeted application.

Backbone

Backbone.js is today's framework of choice, and for good reason; an impressive list of brands, such as Foursquare, Posterous, Groupon (Figure 4-10), and many others have built JavaScript applications with Backbone.

Figure 4-10. Groupon uses Backbone

Backbone uses *Underscore.js* heavily and gives developers the options of using jQuery or Zepto for the core DOM framework. It also boasts a healthy community and strong word of mouth (Figure 4-11).

Figure 4-11. Backbone github stats, June 2012

With Backbone, you represent your data as *models*, which can be created, validated, destroyed, and saved to the server. Whenever a UI action causes an attribute of a model to change, the model triggers a change event; all the views that display the model's state can be notified of the change so that they are able to respond accordingly, rerendering themselves with the new information. In a finished Backbone app, you don't have to write the glue code that looks into the DOM to find an element with a specific ID and update the HTML manually. When the model changes, the views simply update themselves.

In the end, Backbone is better suited for larger frameworks and applications. If you are writing a simple application that needs the structure of MVC, you will end up writing a lot of code to present a simple interface.

 Each framework discussion gives a demo hosted in this book's github repository. For Backbone, you can find the following RESTful demo written in Java at *https://github.com/html5e/backbone-jax-cellar*.

Backbone server synchronization

If your backend data is exposed through a pure RESTful API, retrieving (GET), creating (POST), updating (PUT), and deleting (DELETE) models is incredibly easy using the *Backbone.js* simple Model API. For example:

```
// Models
window.Book = Backbone.Model.extend({
    urlRoot:"/api/books",
    defaults:{
        "id":null,
        "name":"HTML5 Architecture",
    }
});

window.BookCollection = Backbone.Collection.extend({
    model:Book,
    url:"/api/books"
});
```

In the above code, the urlRoot for window.Book is the RESTful service endpoint to retrieve or persist model data. Note that this attribute is needed only when retrieving or persisting models that are not part of a collection. If the Model is part of a *collection*, the url attribute defined in the collection is enough for Backbone to know how to retrieve, update, or delete data using your RESTful API.

In window.BookCollection, url provides the endpoint for the RESTful API. This is all that's needed to retrieve, create, update, and delete with Backbone's simple Model API.

If your persistence layer is not available through RESTful services, or if you would like to use a different transport mechanism such as WebSockets, you can override Backbone.sync.

Backbone.sync is the function that Backbone calls every time it attempts to read or save a model to the server. By default, it uses jQuery or Zepto to make a RESTful JSON request. You can override it to use a different persistence strategy, such as WebSockets, XML transport, or localStorage. With the default implementation, when Backbone.sync sends up a request to save a model, its attributes will be passed, serialized as JSON, and sent in the HTTP body with content-type application/json. The default sync handler maps CRUD to REST like so:

```
create -> POST    /collection
read -> GET    /collection[/id]
update -> PUT    /collection/id
delete -> DELETE    /collection/id
```

Backbone and legacy servers

If you must work with a legacy web server that doesn't support Backbones's default REST/HTTP approach, you may choose to turn on Backbone.emulateHTTP. Setting this option will fake PUT and DELETE requests with a HTTP POST, setting the X-HTTP-Method-Override header with the true method. If emulateJSON is also on, the true method will be passed as an additional _method parameter. For example:

```
Backbone.emulateHTTP = true;
model.save(); // POST to "/collection/id", with "_method=PUT" + header.
```

If you're working with a web server that can't handle requests encoded as application/JSON, setting Backbone.emulateJSON = true; will cause the JSON to be serialized under a model parameter, and the request to be made with a application/x-www-form-urlencoded mime type, as if from an HTML form.

Ember

Ember.js (formerly *Amber.js* and SproutCore 2.0) is one of the newest contenders. It is an attempt to extricate the core features from SproutCore 2.0 into a more compact modular framework suited for the Web. It's also well known for gracefully handling DOM updates and has a respectable following on github (Figure 4-12).

Figure 4-12. Ember github stats, June 2012

Ember is what happened when SproutCore decided to be less Apple Cocoa and more jQuery. The result is a web framework that retains important high-level concepts, such as observers, bindings, and state charts, while delivering a concise API. SproutCore started its life as the development framework behind an early client-side email application. Then, Apple used it to build MobileMe (and then iCloud), both of which include email clients. Needless to say, Apple has figured out that collections that update from the server are very important.

Unlike Backbone, Ember requires less wiring of things together; for example, point a view at an array, and it will automatically be rerendered as the array is manipulated. Ember's binding system and tight integration with the *Handlebars.js* (*http://handle barsjs.com/*) templating language makes this possible.

 For a RESTful demo, written in Ruby, to demonstrate Ember's server synchronization, view this repository: *https://github.com/html5e/ember_data_example*.

Ember server synchronization

Ember Data is a library for loading models from a persistence layer (such as a JSON API), updating those models, and then saving the changes. It provides many of the facilities you find in such server-side ORMs as ActiveRecord, but it is designed specifically for the unique environment of JavaScript in the browser. Here is a brief example of storing data with Ember:

```
// our model
App.Person = Ember.Object.extend();

App.people = Ember.ArrayController.create({
  content: [],
  save: function () {
    // assuming you are using jQuery, but could be other AJAX/DOM framework
    $.post({
```

```
        url: "/people",
        data: JSON.stringify( this.toArray() ),
        success: function ( data ) {
          // your data should already be rendered with latest changes
          // however, you might want to change status from something to "saved" etc.
        }
      });
    }
  });
```

The next step in your code would be a call to `App.people.save()` to persist the data.

Angular

A nice framework developed by Googlers *Angular.js*, has some very interesting design choices, most namely Dependency Injection (or IOC) for JavaScript. *Dependency Injection* makes your code easier to test and pushes object creation and wiring as high up in the application as possible, which gives you one central location for the flow of logic.

Angular is well thought out with respect to template scoping and controller design. It supports a rich UI-binding syntax to make operations like filtering and transforming values easy. On github, Angular is a heavily watched project and has a healthy community contributing to it (Figure 4-13).

Figure 4-13. Angular github stats, June 2012

For a RESTful demo written with *Node.js* to demonstrate Angular's server synchronization capabilities, see *https://github.com/html5e/ angular-phonecat-mongodb-rest*.

Angular server synchronization. The Angular model is referenced from properties on Angular scope objects. The data in your model could be JavaScript objects, arrays, or primitives; it doesn't matter. What matters is that these are all referenced by the scope object. Angular employs scopes to keep your data model and your UI in sync. Whenever something occurs to change the state of the model, Angular immediately reflects that change in the UI and vice versa.

When building web applications, your design needs to consider security threats from JSON vulnerability and XSRF. Both the server and client must cooperate to eliminate these threats. Angular comes preconfigured with strategies that address these issues, but for this to work, backend server cooperation is required.

This simple example illustrates how to retrieve and save data with Angular's default CRUD methods (`.get`, `.save`, `.delete`, and `.query`):

```
// Define CreditCard class
var CreditCard = $resource('/user/:userId/card/:cardId',
 {userId:123, cardId:'@id'}, {
  charge: {method:'POST', params:{charge:true}}
 });

// We can retrieve a collection from the server
var cards = CreditCard.query();
// GET: /user/123/card
// server returns: [ {id:456, number:'1234', name:'Smith'} ];

var card = cards[0];
// each item is an instance of CreditCard
expect(card instanceof CreditCard).toEqual(true);
card.name = "J. Smith";
// non GET methods are mapped onto the instances
card.$save();
// POST: /user/123/card/456 {id:456, number:'1234', name:'J. Smith'}
// server returns: {id:456, number:'1234', name: 'J. Smith'};
```

For more details see:

- *http://docs.angularjs.org/#!/api/angular.service.$xhr*
- *http://docs.angularjs.org/#!/api/angular.service.$resource*

Batman

Created by Shopify, *Batman.js* is another framework similar to Knockout and Angular. It has a nice UI binding system based on HTML attributes and is the only framework written in coffeescript. *Batman.js* is also tightly integrated with *Node.js* and even goes to the extent of having its own (optional) *Node.js* server. At this time, its following is still relatively small on github in comparison to the others (Figure 4-14).

Figure 4-14. Batman github stats, June 2012

For a RESTful application that demonstrates Batman's server synchronization, see the HTML5e Batman repository (*https://github.com/html5e/batmanjs-address-book*).

Batman server synchronization. A *Batman.js* (*http://batmanjs.org/documentation.html#models*) model object may have arbitrary properties set on it, just like any JS object. Only some of those properties are serialized and persisted to its storage backends. Models have the ability to:

- Persist to various storage backends
- Only serialize a defined subset of their properties as JSON
- Use a state machine to expose life cycle events
- Validate with synchronous or asynchronous operations

You define persisted attributes on a model with the encode macro:

```
class Article extends
Batman.Model
    @encode 'body_html', 'title', 'author', 'summary_html', 'blog_id', 'id', 'user_id'
    @encode 'created_at', 'updated_at', 'published_at', Batman.Encoders.railsDate
    @encode 'tags',
      encode: (tagSet) -> tagSet.toArray().join(', ')
      decode: (tagString) -> new Batman.Set(tagString.split(', ')...)
```

Given one or more strings as arguments, @encode will register these properties as persisted attributes of the model, to be serialized in the model's toJSON() output and extracted in its fromJSON(). Properties that aren't specified with @encode will be ignored for both serialization and deserialization. If an optional coder object is provided as the last argument, its encode and decode functions will be used by the Model for serialization and deserialization, respectively.

By default, a model's primary key (the unchanging property that uniquely indexes its instances) is its id property. If you want your model to have a different primary key, specify the name of the key on the primaryKey class property:

```
class User extends
Batman.Model
  @primaryKey: 'handle'
  @encode 'handle', 'email'
```

To specify a storage adapter for persisting a model, use the @persist macro in its class definition:

```
class Product extends
Batman.Model
  @persist Batman.LocalStorage
```

Now when you call `save()` or `load()` on a product, it will use the browser window's `localStorage` to retrieve or store the serialized data.

If you have a REST backend you want to connect to, `Batman.RestStorage` is a simple storage adapter that you can subclass and extend to suit your needs. By default, it assumes your camelcased-singular product model is accessible at the underscored-pluralized /products path, with instances of the resource accessible at /products/:id. You can override these path defaults by assigning either a string or a function-returning a-string to the `url` property of your model class (for the collection path) or to the prototype (for the member path). For example:

```
class Product extends
Batman.Model
  @persist Batman.RestStorage
  @url = "/admin/products"
  url: -> "/admin/products/#{@id}"
```

Knockout

Knockout.js is built around three core features:

- Observables and dependency tracking
- Declarative bindings
- Templating

Knockout is designed to allow the use of arbitrary JavaScript objects as `viewModels`. As long as some of your `viewModel`'s properties are observables, you can use Knockout to bind them to your UI, and the UI will be updated automatically whenever the observable properties change. Figure 4-15 shows Knockout to have a good following of users and commit logs are active.

Figure 4-15. Knockout github stats, June 2012

 For a full demo on how to use Knockout's server synchronization, view this tutorial (*http://learn.knockoutjs.com/#/?tutorial=loadingsaving*).

Knockout server synchronization.   Observables are declared on model properties. They allow automatic updates to the UI when the model changes:

```
var viewModel = {
    serverTime: ko.observable(),
    numUsers: ko.observable()
}
```

Because the server doesn't have any concept of observables, it will just supply a plain JavaScript object (usually serialized as JSON).

You could manually bind this `viewModel` to some HTML elements as follows:

```
The time on the server is: <span
data-bind='text: serverTime'></span>
and <span data-bind='text: numUsers'></span> user(s) are
connected.
```

Because the `viewModel` properties are observable, Knockout will automatically update the HTML elements whenever those properties change.

Next, you want to fetch the latest data from the server. For demo purposes, you might issue an AJAX request every five seconds (perhaps using jQuery's `$.getJSON` or `$.ajax` functions):

```
var data = getDataUsingAjax();
        // Gets the data from the server
```

The server might return JSON data similar to the following:

```
{
    serverTime: '2010-01-07',
    numUsers: 3
}
```

Finally, to update your `viewModel` using this data, you would write:

```
// Every time data is received
from the server:
viewModel.serverTime(data.serverTime);
viewModel.numUsers(data.numUsers);
```

You would have to do this for every variable you want to display on your page. If your data structures become more complex and contain children or arrays, this becomes very cumbersome to handle manually. However, Knockout provides facilities to easily populate a `viewModel` with an incoming JSON payload.

Alternately, you could use the *Knockout.js* mapping plug-in (*http://knockoutjs.com/docu mentation/plugins-mapping.html*). This plug-in allows you to create a mapping from the regular JavaScript object (or JSON structure) to an observable `viewModel`. The mapping plug-in gives you a straightforward way to map that plain JavaScript object into a `view Model` with the appropriate observables. This is an alternative to manually writing your own JavaScript code that constructs a `viewModel` based on some data you've fetched from the server.

To create a `viewModel` via the mapping plug-in, replace the creation of `viewModel` in the code above with the `ko.mapping.fromJS` function:

```
var viewModel =
ko.mapping.fromJS(data);
```

This automatically creates observable properties for each of the properties on data. Then, every time you receive new data from the server, you can update all the properties on `viewModel` in one step by calling the `ko.mapping.fromJS` function again:

```
// Every time data is received
from the server:
ko.mapping.fromJS(data, viewModel);
```

All properties of an object are converted into an observable. If an update would change the value, it will update the observable.

Arrays are converted into observable arrays. If an update would change the number of items, it will perform the appropriate add or remove actions. It will also try to keep the order the same as the original JavaScript array.

## CHAPTER 5

WebSockets

Every HTTP request sent from the browser includes headers, whether you want them or not. Nor are they small headers. Uncompressed request and response headers can vary in size from 200 bytes to over 2K. Although, typical size is somewhere between 700 and 900 bytes, those numbers will grow as userAgents expand features.

WebSockets give you minimal overhead and a much more efficient way of delivering data to the client and server with full duplex communication through a single socket. The WebSocket connection is made after a small HTTP handshake occurs between the client and the server, over the same underlying TCP/IP connection. This gives you an open connection between the client and the server, and both parties can start sending data at any time.

A few of WebSockets' many advantages are:

- No HTTP headers
- No lag due to keep-alive issues
- Low latency, better throughput and responsiveness
- Easier on mobile device batteries

Building the Stack

To effectively develop any application with WebSockets, you must accept the idea of the "real-time Web" in which the client-side code of your web application communicates continuously with a corresponding real-time server during every user connection. To accomplish this, you can use a capable protocol such as WebSockets or SPDY to build the stack yourself. Or you can choose a service or project to manage the connections and graceful degradation for you. In this chapter, you'll learn how to implement a raw WebSocket server and the best practices surrounding the details of setting one up.

If you opt to leave the management to someone else, you have choices. Freemium services, such as Pusher (*http://pusher.com*), are starting to emerge to do this, and companies like Kaazing, which offers the Kaazing Gateway, have been providing adapters for STOMP and Apache ActiveMQ for years. In addition, you can find plenty of wrapper frameworks around WebSockets to provide graceful degradation—from Socket.IO to CometD to whatever's hot right now. Graceful degradation is the process of falling back to use older technologies, such as Flash or long polling, within the browser if the WebSocket protocol is not supported. Comet, push technology, and long-polling in web apps are slow, inefficient, inelegant and have a higher potential magnitude for unreliability. For this book, I am only covering the core WebSocket specification to avoid confusion and to keep things simple.

 As of August 2012, the WebSocket specification was in Working Draft status. Implementers and editors were working to bring the spec into Candidate Release status. Until that status is declared, be aware that things could change in regard to the underlying protocol.

On the Server, Behind the Scenes

Keeping a large number of connections open at the same time requires an architecture that permits other processing to continue before the transmission has finished. Such architectures are usually designed around threading or *asynchronous nonblocking IO* (*NIO*). As for the debates between NIO and threading, some might say that NIO does not actually perform better than threading, but only allows you to write single-threaded event loops for multiple clients as with select on Unix. Others argue that choosing NIO or threading depends on your expected workloads. If you have lots of long-term idle connections, NIO wins due to not having thousands of threads "blocking on a read" operation. Again, there are many debates over whether threads are faster or easier to write than event loops (or the opposite) so it all depends on the type of use case you are trying to handle. Don't worry, I'll show examples of both event loops and threads in this chapter.

Programming Models

As mentioned earlier, WebSockets present a new development model for server- and client-side applications: the "real-time" Web. During every user connection under this model, your web application's client side needs to communicate continuously with the corresponding real-time server. Although most server-side frameworks provide eventing mechanisms, few extend the events all the way through to the web browser to support this real-time model. As a result, you are faced with retrofitting your current solutions and architectures into this real-time model.

For example, suppose your server-side framework is capable of sending an event and you have observers of this event in your code. WebSockets gives you the ability to extend that event so that it carries all the way from the server side into the connected client's browser. A good example would be to notify all WebSocket connections that a user has registered on your site.

The first step towards implementing such a solution is to wire up the three main listeners associated with WebSockets: onopen, onmessage, and onclose. Basically, the following events will be fired automatically when a WebSocket connection opens successfully. For example:

```
objWebSocket.onopen = function(evt)
{
    alert("WebSocket connection opened successfully");
};
objWebSocket.onmessage = function(evt)
{
    alert("Message : " + evt.data);
};
objWebSocket .onclose = function(evt)
{
    alert("WebSocket connection closed");
};
```

After the WebSocket connection opens, the onmessage event fires whenever the server sends data to the client. If the client wants to send data to the server, it can do so as follows:

```
objWebSocket.send("Hello World");
```

Sending messages in the form of strings over raw WebSockets isn't very appealing, however, when you want to develop enterprise-style web applications. Because current WebSocket implementations deal mostly with strings, you can use JSON to transfer data to and from the server.

But how do you propagate the server-side events that are fired on the server and then bubble them up on the client? One approach is to relay the events. When a specific server-side event is fired, use a listener or observer to translate the data to JSON and send it to all connected clients.

Relaying Events from the Server to the Browser

Before you can successfully communicate with a server, you need to know what you're talking to and how. For the chapter's examples, I'm using the JBoss AS7 application server (*http://www.jboss.org/jbossas/downloads*) and embedding Jetty within the web application. The main reasoning behind this approach is to take advantage of a lightweight Java EE 6.0 [Full Profile] application server. There are a few other Java options out there, such as GlassFish or running Jetty standalone, but this solution offers contexts and dependency injection (CDI), distributed transactions, scalable JMS messaging, and data grid support out of the box. Such support is extremely valuable in cutting-edge enterprise initiatives and private cloud architectures.

Because this approach embeds one server (Jetty) with another server (JBoss), we can use it with any app server, even one that may not support WebSockets, and enable existing, older applications to take advantage of real-time connections.

The full deployable source code for this example is on the "embedded-jetty branch (*https://github.com/html5e/HTML5-Mobile-WebSocket/tree/embedded-jetty*)". A few things are worth noting here:

Security
> Because the WebSocket server is running on a different port (8081) than the JBoss AS7 server (8080), we must account for not having authentication cookies, and so on. A reverse proxy can handle this problem, however, as you'll see in the last section of this chapter.

Proxies
> As if existing proxy servers weren't already a huge problem for running WebSockets and HTTP over the same port, in this example, we are now running them separately.

Threading
> Because we're observing and listening for CDI events, we must perform some same thread operations and connection sharing.

The code below first sets up the WebSocket server using Jetty's `WebSocketHandler` and embeds it inside a `ServletContextListener`. Although the app shares a synchronized set of WebSocket connections across threads, we ensure that only a single thread can execute a method or block at one time by using the `synchronized` keyword. To relay the CDI event to the browser, we must store all the WebSocket connections in a `Concur rentHashSet` and write new connections to it as they come online. At any time, the `ConcurrentHashSet` will be read on a different thread so we know where to relay the CDI events. The `ChatWebSocketHandler` contains a global set of WebSocket connections and adds each new connection within the Jetty server.

```
public class ChatWebSocketHandler extends WebSocketHandler {

private static Set<ChatWebSocket> websockets =
    new ConcurrentHashSet<ChatWebSocket>();

    public WebSocket doWebSocketConnect(HttpServletRequest request,
            String protocol) {
        return new ChatWebSocket();
```

```
            }

        public class ChatWebSocket implements WebSocket.OnTextMessage {

            private Connection connection;

            public void onOpen(Connection connection) {
                // Client (Browser) WebSockets has opened a connection.
                // 1) Store the opened connection
                this.connection = connection;
                // 2) Add ChatWebSocket in the global list of ChatWebSocket
                // instances
                // instance.
                getWebsockets().add(this);
            }

            public void onMessage(String data) {
                // Loop for each instance of ChatWebSocket to send message
                // server to each client WebSockets.
                try {
                    for (ChatWebSocket webSocket : getWebsockets()) {
                        // send a message to the current client WebSocket.
                        webSocket.connection.sendMessage(data);
                    }
                } catch (IOException x) {
                    // Error was detected, close the ChatWebSocket client side
                    this.connection.disconnect();
                }

            }

            public void onClose(int closeCode, String message) {
                // Remove ChatWebSocket in the global list of ChatWebSocket
                // instance.
                getWebsockets().remove(this);
            }
        }

        public static synchronized Set<ChatWebSocket> getWebsockets() {
            return websockets;
        }

    }
```

Next, we embed the Jetty WebSocket-capable server within the web application:

```
    private Server server = null;
    /**
     * Start Embedding Jetty server when WEB Application is started.
     *
     */
    public void contextInitialized(ServletContextEvent event) {
        try {
```

```
// 1) Create a Jetty server with the 8081 port.
InetAddress addr = InetAddress.getLocalHost();
this.server = new Server();
Connector connector = new SelectChannelConnector();
connector.setPort(8081);
connector.setHost(addr.getHostAddress());

server.addConnector(connector);

// 2) Register ChatWebSocketHandler in the
//Jetty server instance.
ChatWebSocketHandler chatWebSocketHandler =
                        new ChatWebSocketHandler();
chatWebSocketHandler.setHandler(new DefaultHandler());

server.setHandler(chatWebSocketHandler);

// 2) Start the Jetty server.
server.start();
    } catch (Throwable e) {
        e.printStackTrace();
    }
}

....
}
```

Now we'll create a method to observe CDI events and send the fired `Member` events to all active connections. This relays a very simple `cdievent` JavaScript object, which will be pushed to all connected clients and then evaluated on the browser through a JavaScript interpreter.

```
public void observeItemEvent(@Observes Member member) {
        try {
            for (ChatWebSocket webSocket : websockets) {

webSocket.connection.sendMessage("{\"cdievent\":{\"fire\":function(){" +
                    "eventObj.initEvent(\'memberEvent\', true, true);" +
                    "eventObj.name = '" + member.getName() + "';\n" +
                    "document.dispatchEvent(eventObj);" +
                    "}}}");
            }
        } catch (IOException x) {
            //...
        }
    }
```

The above code observes the following event when a new `Member` is registered through the web interface. As you can see below, `memberEventSrc.fire(member)` is fired when a user registers through the provided RESTful URL.

```
@POST
@Consumes(MediaType.APPLICATION_FORM_URLENCODED)
@Produces(MediaType.APPLICATION_JSON)
public Response createMember(@FormParam("name") String name,
                             @FormParam("email") String email,
                             @FormParam("phoneNumber") String phone) {
    ...

        //Create a new member class from fields
        Member member = new Member();
        member.setName(name);
        member.setEmail(email);
        member.setPhoneNumber(phone);

        try {

            //Fire the CDI event
            memberEventSrc.fire(member);
```

Finally, we set up the WebSocket JavaScript client and safely avoid using the eval()
method to execute the received JavaScript.

```
        ...
        var location = "ws://192.168.1.101:8081/"
        this._ws = new WebSocket(location);
        ....
        _onmessage : function(m) {
            if (m.data) {
                //check to see if this message is a CDI event
                if(m.data.indexOf('cdievent') > 0){
                    try{
                        //$('log').innerHTML = m.data;
                        //avoid use of eval...
                        var event = (m.data);
                        event = (new Function("return " + event))();
                        event.cdievent.fire();
                    }catch(e){
                        alert(e);
                    }
                }else{
                    //... append data in the DOM
                }
            }
        },
```

Here is the JavaScript code that listens for the CDI event and executes the necessary
client-side code:

```
window.addEventListener('memberEvent', function(e) {
    alert(e.name + ' just registered!');
}, false);
```

As you can see, this is a very prototyped approach to achieve a running WebSocket server, but it's a step forward in adding a usable programming layer on top of the WebSocket protocol.

Using the new and shiny

As of this writing, JBoss has just begun to implement WebSockets natively on JBoss AS7. The same example from above has been converted for native WebSocket support (without embedding Jetty) on JBoss AS 7.1.2 and beyond. This gives you the benefit of having both HTTP and WS traffic over the same port without needing to worry about managing data across threads. To see a chat room example that uses native WebSocket, check out *https://github.com/html5e/HTML5-Mobile-WebSocket*. You can find the JBoss WebSocket source at *https://github.com/mikebrock/jboss-websockets*.

Binary Data Over WebSockets

Another cool use of WebSockets is the ability to use binary data instead of just JSON strings. For example:

```
objWebSocket.onopen = function(evt)
{
    var array = new Float32Array(5);
    for (var i = 0; i < array.length; ++i) array[i] = i / 2;
    ws.send(array, {binary: true});
};
```

Why send binary data? This allows you to stream audio to connected clients using the Web Audio API. Or you could give users the ability to collaborate with a real-time screen sharing application using canvas and avoid the need to base64-encode the images. The possibilities are limitless!

The following code sets up a *Node.js* server to demo an example of sending audio over a WebSocket connection. See *https://github.com/einaros/ws-audio-example* for the full example.

```
var express = require('express');
var WebSocketServer = require('ws').Server;
var app = express.createServer();

function getSoundBuffer(samples) {
  var header = new Buffer([
      0x52,0x49,0x46,0x46, // "RIFF"
      0, 0, 0, 0,          // put total size here
      0x57,0x41,0x56,0x45, // "WAVE"
      0x66,0x6d,0x74,0x20, // "fmt "
      16,0,0,0,            // size of the following
      1, 0,                // PCM format
      1, 0,                // Mono: 1 channel
      0x44,0xAC,0,0,       // 44,100 samples per second
```

```
      0x88,0x58,0x01,0,      // byte rate: two bytes per sample
      2, 0,                  // aligned on every two bytes
      16, 0,                 // 16 bits per sample
      0x64,0x61,0x74,0x61,   // "data"
      0, 0, 0, 0             // put number of samples here
  ]);
  header.writeUInt32LE(36 + samples.length, 4, true);
  header.writeUInt32LE(samples.length, 40, true);
  var data = new Buffer(header.length + samples.length);
  header.copy(data);
  samples.copy(data, header.length);
  return data;
}

function makeSamples(frequency, duration) {
  var samplespercycle = 44100 / frequency;
  var samples = new Uint16Array(44100 * duration);
  var da = 2 * Math.PI / samplespercycle;
  for (var i = 0, a = 0; i < samples.length; i++, a += da) {
    samples[i] = Math.floor(Math.sin(a / 300000) * 32768);
  }
  return
getSoundBuffer(new Buffer(Array.prototype.slice.call(samples, 0)));
}

app.use(express.static(__dirname + '/public'));
app.listen(8080);
var wss = new WebSocketServer({server: app, path: '/data'});

var samples = makeSamples(20000, 10);

wss.on('connection', function(ws) {
  ws.on('message', function(message) {
    ws.send('pong');
  });
  ws.send(samples, {binary: true});
});
```

Managing Proxies

With new technology comes a new set of problems. In the case of WebSockets, the challenges relate to compatibility with the proxy servers that mediate HTTP connections in most company networks. A firewall, proxy server, or switch always is the lynchpin of an enterprise, and these devices and servers limit the kind of traffic you're allowed to send to and from the server.

The WebSocket protocol uses the HTTP upgrade system (which is normally used for HTTPS/SSL) to "upgrade" an HTTP connection to a WebSocket connection. Some proxy servers are not able to handle this handshake and will drop the connection. So, even if a given client uses the WebSocket protocol, it may not be possible to establish a connection.

> When you use WebSocket Secure (*wss://*), wire traffic is encrypted and intermediate transparent proxy servers may simply allow the encrypted traffic through, so there is a much better chance that the WebSocket connection will succeed. Using encryption is not free of resource costs, but often provides the highest success rate.

Some proxy servers are harmless and work fine with WebSockets. Others will prevent WebSockets from working correctly, causing the connection to fail. In some cases, additional proxy server configuration may be required, and certain proxy servers may need to be upgraded to support WebSocket connections.

If unencrypted WebSocket traffic flows through an explicit or a transparent proxy server on its way to the WebSocket server, then, whether or not the proxy server behaves as it should, the connection is almost certainly bound to fail. Therefore, unencrypted Web-Socket connections should be used only in the simplest topologies. As WebSockets become more mainstream, proxy servers will become WebSocket aware.

If you use an encrypted WebSocket connection, then use *Transport Layer Security* (*TLS*) in the WebSocket Secure connection to ensure that an HTTP CONNECT command is issued when the browser is configured to use an explicit proxy server. This sets up a tunnel, which provides low-level end-to-end TCP communication through the HTTP proxy, between the WebSocket Secure client and the WebSocket server. In the case of transparent proxy servers, the browser is unaware of the proxy server, so no HTTP CONNECT is sent. Because the wire traffic is encrypted, however, intermediate transparent proxy servers may simply allow the encrypted traffic through, so there is a much better chance that the WebSocket connection will succeed if you use WebSocket Secure. Using encryption is not free of resource cost, but often provides the highest success rate.

> A mid-2010 draft (version hixie-76) broke compatibility with reverse proxies and gateways by including 8 bytes of key data after the headers, but not advertising that data in a Content-Length: 8 header. This data was not forwarded by all intermediates, which could lead to protocol failure. More recent drafts (such as hybi-09) put the key data in a Sec-WebSocket-Key header, solving this problem.

Building your own

Things have changed since the days of fronting our servers with Apache for tasks like static resource serving. Apache configuration changes result in killing hundreds of active connections, which in turn, kills service availability.

With today's private cloud architectures, there is a high demand for throughput and availability. If we want our services like Apache or Tomcat to come up or go down at any time, then we simply have to put something in front of those services that can handle routing the traffic correctly, based on the cloud topology at the moment. One way to take down servers and bring up new ones without affecting service availability is to use a proxy. In most cases, HAProxy is the go to-choice for high throughput and availability.

HAProxy is a lightweight proxy server that advertises obscenely high throughput. Such companies as github, Fedora, Stack Overflow, and Twitter all use HAProxy for load balancing and scaling their infrastructure. Not only can HAProxy handle HTTP traffic, but it's also a general-purpose TCP/IP proxy. Best of all, it's dead simple to use.

The code that follows adds HAProxy to the previous example. The result is a reverse proxy on the WebSocket port (8081), which allows all traffic (HTTP and WS) to be sent across a common port (8080, in this case). Here is a simple reverse proxy from the example WebSocket server:

```
global
    maxconn     4096 # Total Max Connections. This is dependent on ulimit
    nbproc      1

defaults
    mode        http

frontend all 0.0.0.0:8080
    timeout client 86400000
    default_backend www_backend
    acl is_websocket hdr(Upgrade) -i WebSocket
    acl is_websocket hdr_beg(Host) -i ws

    use_backend socket_backend if is_websocket

backend www_backend
    balance roundrobin
    option forwardfor # This sets X-Forwarded-For
    timeout server 30000
    timeout connect 4000
    server apiserver 192.168.1.101:8080 weight 1 maxconn 4096 check

backend socket_backend
    balance roundrobin
    option forwardfor # This sets X-Forwarded-For
```

```
timeout queue 5000
timeout server 86400000
timeout connect 86400000
server apiserver 192.168.1.101:8081 weight 1 maxconn 4096 check
```

This approach is universal to any HTTP server that embeds a separate WebSocket server on a different port.

Frameworks

There are just about as many Comet, AJAX push-based, WebSocket frameworks and servers as there are mobile web frameworks. So sorting out which ones are built for lightweight mobile environments and which ones may be suitable only for desktop browsers is essential. Keep in mind that graceful degradation comes at a cost. If you choose a WebSocket framework that degrades in 10 different ways, you do not want your mobile clients to be penalized with a heavy framework download. To provide real-time connectivity to every browser, you need a framework that will detect the most capable transport at runtime.

You may already be familiar with projects such as *Node.js*, Ruby EventMachine, or Python Twisted. These projects use an event-based API to allow you to create network-aware applications in just a few lines of code. But what about enterprise-grade performance and concurrency? Take a look at how a few of your options stack up.

Vert.x

A fully asynchronous, general-purpose application container for JVM languages, Vert.x (*https://github.com/vert-x/vert.x*)) takes inspiration from such event-driven frameworks as *Node.js*, then combines it with a distributed event bus and sticks it all on the JVM. The result is a runtime with *real* concurrency and unrivalled performance. Vert.x then exposes the API in Ruby, JavaScript, Groovy, and Java. Vert.x supports TCP, HTTP, WebSockets, and many more modules. You can think of it as *Node.js* for JVM languages.

Vert.x recommends SockJS to provide a WebSocket-like object on the client. Under the hood, SockJS tries to use native WebSockets first. If that fails, it can use a variety of browser-specific transport protocols and presents them through WebSocket-like abstractions. SockJS is intended to work for all modern browsers and in environments that don't support WebSocket protcol, such as behind restrictive corporate proxies.

Vert.x requires JDK 1.7.0. It uses such open source projects as Netty, JRuby, Mozilla Rhino, and Hazelcast, and is under MIT and Apache 2.0 license.

The code for SockJS page set-up is:

```
<!DOCTYPE html>
<html>
<head>
    <title>my app</title>
```

```
  </head>
  <body>
    <script src="http://cdn.sockjs.org/sockjs-0.1.min.js"></script>
  </body>
</html>
```

To use SockJS:

```
var sock = new SockJS('http://mydomain.com/my_prefix');
    sock.onopen = function() {
        console.log('open');
    };
    sock.onmessage = function(e) {
        console.log('message', e.data);
    };
    sock.onclose = function() {
        console.log('close');
    };
```

Socket.IO

Specifically built for use with a *Node.js* server, Socket.IO (*http://socket.io*) has the capability to be used with any backend after you set fallback capabilities via Flash. Socket.IO aims to make real-time apps possible in every browser and mobile device, blurring the differences between the different transport mechanisms. Specifically, Socket.IO supports iOS, Android, WebOs, and WebKit License, and is under MIT license.

The page setup for Socket.IO is simple:

```
<!DOCTYPE html>
<html>
<head>
    <title>my app</title>
</head>
<body>
    <script src="http://cdn.socket.io/stable/socket.io.js"></script>
</body>
</html>
```

To set up a server, use:

```
var io = require('socket.io').listen(80);

io.sockets.on('connection', function (socket) {
  socket.emit('news', { hello: 'world' });
  socket.on('my other event', function (data) {
    console.log(data);
  });
});
```

Finally, set up your client with:

```
var socket = io.connect('http://localhost');
  socket.on('news', function (data) {
    console.log(data);
    socket.emit('my other event', { my: 'data' });
  });
```

Atmosphere

Atmosphere is the only portable WebSocket/Comet framework supporting Scala, Groovy, and Java. Atmosphere (*https://github.com/Atmosphere*) can run on any Java-based web server, including Tomcat, Jetty, GlassFish, Weblogic, Grizzly, JBoss, Resin, and more. The Atmosphere framework has both client (JavaScript, iQuery, GWT) and server components. You can find many examples of how to use Atmosphere in your project at *https://github.com/Atmosphere/atmosphere/tree/master/samples* (Figure 5-1).

The main concern when using WebSockets is graceful degradation, because most mobile browsers and servers have mixed support. All the frameworks mentioned (plus many more) support some kind of fallback when WebSockets is not available within the browser. All of these fallbacks, however, share the same problem: they carry the overhead of HTTP, which doesn't make them well suited for low-latency mobile applications. Until all mobile browsers support WebSockets, this is a problem users and developers are forced to deal with.

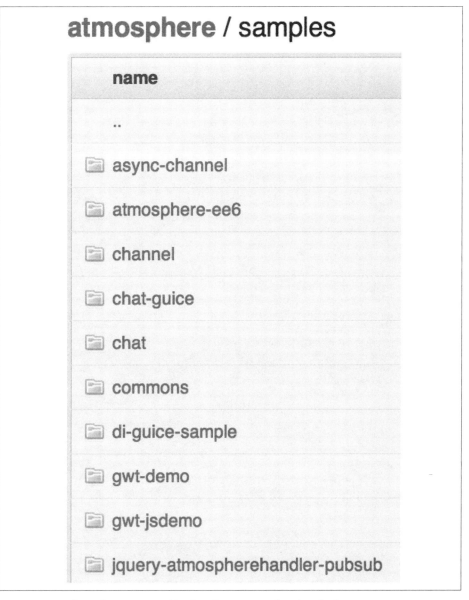

Figure 5-1. A few of many examples listed in Atmosphere's github repo

## CHAPTER 6

Optimizing with Web Storage

Today, you have two widespread and well-supported mechanisms for storing data on the client: cookies and Web Storage. Many say that Web Storage is the evolution of cookies, but in reality, cookies may stick around a lot longer than people think. Mainly because they are much different than Web Storage and implicitly send data back to the server upon each request through HTTP headers. Cookies are always available on the server and can be read and written to freely, which is great for user session management and similar situations. The downside is that you only get 4kb of storage per cookie.

Web Storage is different from cookies in that the stored data is not shared with the server. You can currently store 5MB of data on the client device with Web Storage, and some browsers allow up to 10MB of storage with user approval. However, these limits can be a little misleading. If you try to store 5MB of pure HTML in local storage within WebKit-based browsers, such as Mobile Safari, you will see that it allows for a maximum of 2.6MB only. For this, you can thank section 7.4 of the first W3C Working Draft of the Web Storage specification, which states:

> In general, it is recommended that `userAgent`s not support features that control how databases are stored on disk. For example, there is little reason to allow Web authors to control the character encoding used in the disk representation of the data, as all data in JavaScript is implicitly UTF-16.

Although section 7.4 was removed in following drafts, most WebKit browser vendors have stuck to the UTF-16 implementation of data encoding. Two exceptions, Firefox and IE, give you the actual 5MB of storage space.

Web Storage offers two storage objects—`localStorage` and `sessionStorage`—both of which are widely supported from IE8 upward and in all modern browsers, including mobile devices. (For browsers that don't support Web Storage natively, it includes several polyfills.) Both storage objects use exactly the same APIs, which means that anything you can do with `localStorage`, you can also do with `sessionStorage` and vice versa. With `sessionStorage`, however, your data is stored only while that particular browser window (or tab) is open. After the user closes the window, the data is purged. With `localStorage`, your data will stay on the client across browser sessions, device restart, and more. Any data stored is tied to the document origin, in that it's tied to the specific protocol like HTTP or HTTPS, the top-level domain (for example html5e.org (*http://html5e.org/*)), and the port, usually port 80. One more caveat regarding `sessionStorage`: if the browser supports resuming sessions after restart, then your `sessionStorage` object may be persisted unknowingly. This can be an issue if your use case expects the `sessionStorage` data to be destroyed upon closing of the browser.

Web Storage defines two APIs, Storage and StorageEvent, which either local or session storage can use. This means you have two ways of working with and managing local data. Whichever API you choose, remember with Web Storage, operations are synchronous: When you store or retrieve data, you are blocking the main UI thread, and the rest of the page won't render until your data operations are finished.

The Storage API

As this usage example illustrates, the Storage API offers multiple ways of working with your data in a storage object:

```
localStorage.bookName = 'HTML5 Architecture';
//or
localStorage['bookName'] = 'HTML5 Architecture';
//or
localStorage.setItem('bookName') = 'HTML5 Architecture';
```

You can treat your data like any other JavaScript object and add the key directly as a `localStorage` property, which calls `setItem()` behind the scenes. Your available functions are:

```
.length //returns the number of key/value pairs
.key(n) //returns the name of the nth key in the list
.getItem(key) //returns the current value associated with the key
.setItem(key, value) //creates new or adds to existing key
.removeItem(key) //you can probably guess what this does :)
.clear() //removes everything from storage associated with this domain
```

You might think that all of the methods for storing data have the same performance, but that would be crazy talk in web browser land, right? Figure 6-1 and Figure 6-2 provide a more realistic view and a performance analysis (*http://jsperf.com/localstorage-getitem-setitem-vs-getter-setter/4*) on which storage approach works the best.

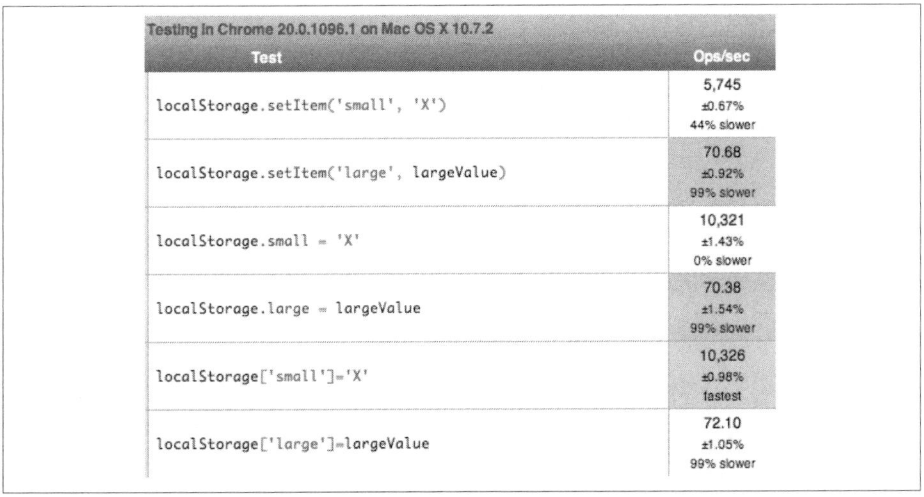

Test	Ops/sec
Testing in Chrome 20.0.1096.1 on Mac OS X 10.7.2	
`localStorage.setItem('small', 'X')`	5,745 ±0.67% 44% slower
`localStorage.setItem('large', largeValue)`	70.68 ±0.92% 99% slower
`localStorage.small = 'X'`	10,321 ±1.43% 0% slower
`localStorage.large = largeValue`	70.38 ±1.54% 99% slower
`localStorage['small']='X'`	10,326 ±0.98% fastest
`localStorage['large']=largeValue`	72.10 ±1.05% 99% slower

Figure 6-1. Chrome performance test

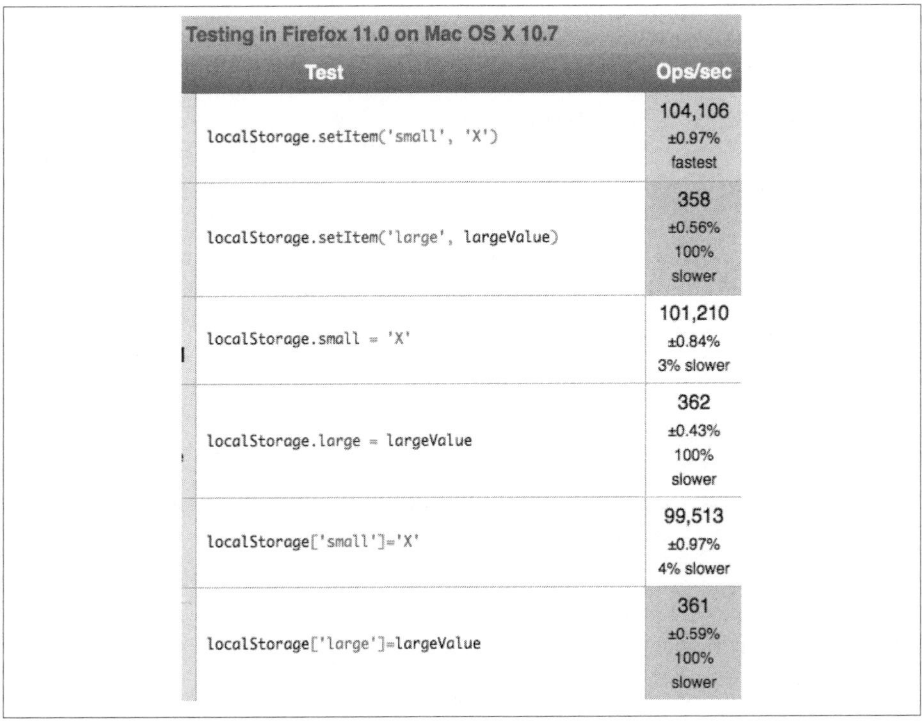

Test	Ops/sec
Testing in Firefox 11.0 on Mac OS X 10.7	
`localStorage.setItem('small', 'X')`	104,106 ±0.97% fastest
`localStorage.setItem('large', largeValue)`	358 ±0.56% 100% slower
`localStorage.small = 'X'`	101,210 ±0.84% 3% slower
`localStorage.large = largeValue`	362 ±0.43% 100% slower
`localStorage['small']='X'`	99,513 ±0.97% 4% slower
`localStorage['large']=largeValue`	361 ±0.59% 100% slower

Figure 6-2. Firefox performance test

Instead of using `localStorage.setItem()` and calling the object setter property directly, with `localStorage.small` or `localStorage['small']`, you can give your data storage a 50% speed boost in Chrome (Figure 6-1). The same performance test in the latest Firefox and Safari web browsers, however, reveals that `localStorage.setItem()` performs better than the others for small values (Figure 6-2).

As for most applications, you want your web app to perform at top speed across all browsers. Usually, a real-world application will store a larger JSON object, base64 image string, or HTML snippet in `localStorage`. As you can see with the `largeValue` tests in the figures, all Storage API options perform roughly the same.

The StorageEvent API

Although Web Storage is considered to be "racy" (more on this in a moment), you can avoid most race conditions by using the StorageEvent API. If the user has the same site open in different tabs, this event can be used to synchronize the data. Here's a sample usage:

```
window.addEventListener('storage', function(evt){alert(evt.key)}, false);

.key //returns the value of the key being changed. It's null upon creation.
.oldValue //represents the old value of the key being changed
.newValue //represents the new value of the key being changed
.url //the address of the document whose key changed
.storageArea //the Storage object which was affected. Either localStorage or sessionStorage
```

The `storage` event is fired only when the new value is not the same as the old value. The `storage` event contains the key, `oldValue`, and `newValue` properties of data that has changed, which you can access in code. This example creates the appropriate event listener, which logs the `oldValue` and `newValue` across all open browser sessions:

```
window.addEventListener('storage', function(event) {
  console.log('The value for ' + event.key + ' was changed from' + event.oldValue
                                         + ' to ' + event.newValue);
}, false);
```

 The `storage` event fires on the other windows only. It won't fire on the window that did the storing.

What's Racy and What's Not?

Ultimately, a downside of Web Storage is the lack of transactions. For example, a user might have your app open in two tabs. Tab 1 starts writing several things to the database, then tab 2 starts reading it, getting the data when it has only partially been updated.

Thus, Web Storage is *racy*, meaning it's susceptible to race conditions. As a result, you need to take precautions to ensure the integrity of your data and the accuracy of any queries. As mentioned earlier, the only mechanism to prevent race conditions is the StorageEvent.

Race conditions can occur with multithreaded browsers, as well, because threads can cause problems when saving data. Here's a good example:

```
var myarray = [a,b];
var first = myarray.splice(0,1);
localStorage.first = first;
```

You would expect the following:

```
localStorage.first == a; //true
```

When a race condition occurs, we could find that this happens:

```
localStorage.first == b; //true
```

As one thread splices `myarray` and is de-scheduled, another thread runs the same code segment and effectively reads `myarray` as only having one element, b, and as such, assigns it to first.

Bottom line, the exact same problem exists with cookies, which doesn't seem to have bothered people much. If race conditions are a problem (or you think they're going to be a problem), you need a more advanced storage mechanism than Web Storage, such as IndexedDB or a solution that can support transactions and write-locks.

Using JSON to Encode and Decode

To store a JavaScript object (or an array perhaps) in your `localStorage` or `session Storage`, you need to use JSON to encode and decode your data, as in:

```
var mydata = {
    "Book" : "HTML5 Architecture",
    "Author" : "Wesley Hales",
};
```

Next, store the JavaScript object as a string:

```
localStorage.setItem("mydata", JSON.stringify(mydata));
```

When you're ready to retrieve the data, use:

```
JSON.parse(localStorage.getItem("mydata"));
```

Security and Private Browsing

All this communication between client and server raises security issues. They come in two flavors: keeping your app secure and private browsing by users.

Because of the potential for DNS spoofing attacks, you cannot guarantee that a host claiming to be in a certain domain really is from that domain. To mitigate this and keep your app secure, you can use *TLS* (*Transport Layer Security*) for your pages. TLS and its predecessor, *Secure Sockets Layer* (*SSL*), are cryptographic protocols that provide communication security over the Internet. Pages using TLS can be sure that only the user, software working on behalf of the user, and other pages using TLS that have certificates identifying them as being from the same domain, can access their storage areas.

Security

Web Storage, both `localStorage` and `sessionStorage`, is not secure and is stored in plain text with no way to encrypt. If you're worried about data security, don't use `local Storage`. There are solutions like JCryption (*http://www.jcryption.org*) for those unwilling to buy SSL certificates or with hosting providers who do not support SSL. It's no replacement for SSL, because there is no authentication, but the jCryption plug-in offers a base level of security while being very easy and quick to install.

 Be aware that any form of JavaScript encryption is intrinsically vulnerable to man-in-the-middle (MITM) attacks, so it is not a recommended practice for storing sensitive data.

Private Browsing

Within certain browsers, while the user is running in private or incognito browsing modes, your application will get an exception when trying to store anything in Web Storage. Every app that uses `localStorage` should check `window['localStorage'].se tItem` for a rising `QUOTA_EXCEEDED_ERR` exception before using it. For example, the problem in Figure 6-3 is that the `window` object still exposes `localStorage` in the global namespace, but when you call `setItem`, this exception is thrown. Any calls to `.remov eItem` are ignored.

> **All** | Errors   Warnings   Logs
> ⊗ QUOTA_EXCEEDED_ERR: DOM Exception   *:4242/storage/:13*
>   22: An attempt was made to add something to storage
>   that exceeded the quota.
> >

Figure 6-3. Error when accessing localStorage

Safari returns null for any item that is set within the `localStorage` or `sessionStor age` objects. So even if you set something before the user goes into private browsing mode, you won't be able to retrieve until they come out of the private session.

Chrome and Opera will allow you to retrieve items set before going into incognito mode, but once private browsing commences, `localStorage` is treated like `sessionStorage` (only items set on the `localStorage` by that session will be returned).

Firefox, like Chrome, will not retrieve items set on `localStorage` prior to a private session starting, but in private browsing treats `localStorage` like `sessionStorage`.

To be safe, always do a series of checks before using `localStorage` or `sessionStorage`:

```
function isLocalStorageSupported() {
    try {
        var supported = ('localStorage' in window &&
                         window['localStorage'] !== null);
        if (supported) {
          localStorage.setItem("storage", "");
          localStorage.removeItem("storage");
        }
        return supported;
    } catch(err) { return false; }
}
```

Who's Using Web Storage?

Take a look at Table 6-1, an overview of the five most visited sites on the Internet, to get an idea of which sites are (or aren't) using Web Storage to optimize.

Table 6-1. Web Storage Survey

Website	Desktop	Mobile
Google Search	Yes, 87K	Yes, 160K
Yahoo!	No	No
Wikipedia	No	No
Twitter	Yes, less than 1K	Yes, 46K
Amazon	Yes, less than 1K	No

For mobile, Google's basic search page is making the most use of `localStorage` by storing base64 images and other CSS. For each subsequent page request, it uses Java-Script to insert `<style>` blocks just after the page title in the document head with the CSS values from `localStorage` (Figure 6-4).

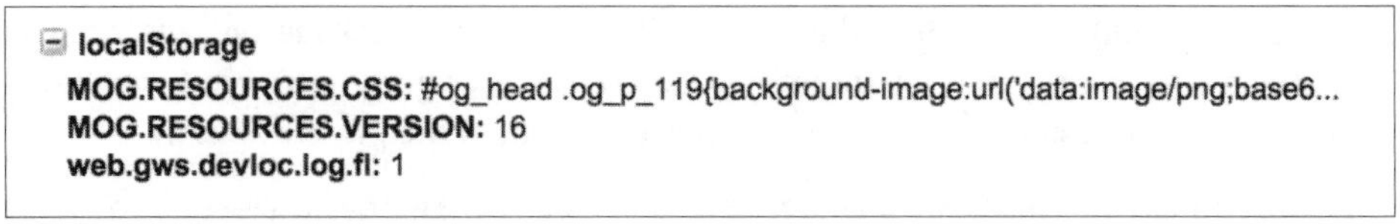

⊟ **localStorage**
  MOG.RESOURCES.CSS: #og_head .og_p_119{background-image:url('data:image/png;base6...
  MOG.RESOURCES.VERSION: 16
  web.gws.devloc.log.fl: 1

Figure 6-4. Google's use of localStorage on mobile

For a basic Google search on the desktop, data is stored differently than on mobile. First, sessionStorage is used, so you know this will be temporary data. Looking at the raw JSON data stored by a simple Google search in Figure 6-5, you can see mostly CSS and HTML is stored along with some namespaced tracking data.

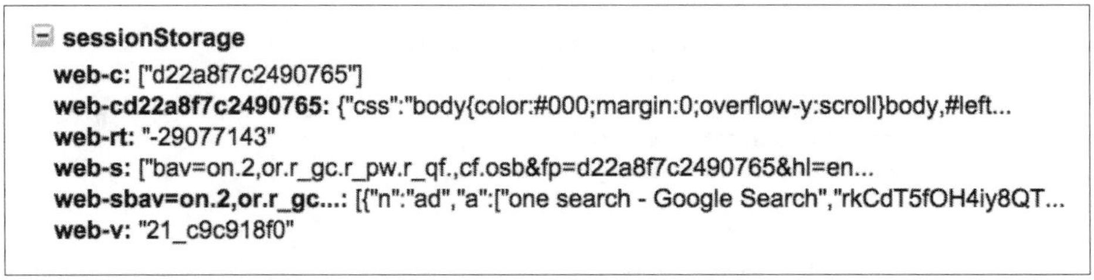

⊟ **sessionStorage**
  web-c: ["d22a8f7c2490765"]
  web-cd22a8f7c2490765: {"css":"body{color:#000;margin:0;overflow-y:scroll}body,#left...
  web-rt: "-29077143"
  web-s: ["bav=on.2,or.r_gc.r_pw.r_qf.,cf.osb&fp=d22a8f7c2490765&hl=en...
  web-sbav=on.2,or.r_gc...: [{"n":"ad","a":["one search - Google Search","rkCdT5fOH4iy8QT...
  web-v: "21_c9c918f0"

Figure 6-5. Google's use of sessionStorage on desktop

Twitter also makes heavy use of localStorage on mobile devices. Looking at the JSON saved on the device in Figure 6-6, you can see that Twitter stores all of the data required to present the user interface. The data isn't a straight dump of HTML to localStor age, however, it's organized in a JSON object structure with proper escaping and Java-Script templating variables.

⊟ **localStorage**
  TWITTER: {"strs":{"connect_followed_by_one":"<span class='highlight'>{...
  onslyde: {"profile":{"retweets":null,"blocking":"false","url":"http://...

Figure 6-6. Twitter's use of localStorage on mobile

Amazon's use of sessionStorage is minimal tracking information related to "product likes." But overall, it's a bit surprising to see that the top sites on the Internet are still not leveraging Web Storage to speed up their site and reduce HTTP requests.

Efficient requests and zippier interfaces may not be a huge problem for desktop sites, but there's no reason we shouldn't have these storage enhancements on both mobile and desktop. Some of the reasons we're seeing heavy Web Storage usage only on mobile are:

- Data URIs (base64 encoding background images) used in CSS work with modern browsers only. There are limits and annoyances with this technique all the way up through IE9.

- Mobile latencies are much higher (as you saw in Chapter 3), so caching on mobile devices can make the UI much faster.

 When using base64-encoded data URIs, be aware that the encoded data is one third larger in size than its binary equivalent. (However, this overhead is reduced to 2 to 3% if the HTTP server compresses the response using GZIP.)

Using Web Storage Today

As you have seen, there are a million different ways to use Web Storage within your application. It really comes down to answering a few questions:

- How can I make the user experience better?
- How can I reduce HTTP requests on mobile?
- How can I efficiently reduce load on the server?

Of course, after seeing that Web Storage blocks the main JavaScript UI thread when accessing data, you must be considerate of how your page loads and use best practices for storing and retrieving data.

The best place to start with localStorage is using it where your app requires user input. For example, if you have a comments input box within a form, you could use local Storage to save a draft on the user input in case the session times out or the form is submitted improperly. The commenting service Disqus follows this practice and saves your draft comments in localStorage.

Enable automatic sign-in

Another good use of localStorage is for automatic sign-in. Here is a recommendation from section 3.3.2 in the W3C Mobile Web Application Best Practices:

> 3.3.2.1 What it means
>
> If an application requires user identity it is usual to prompt for user credentials (username and password) and provide the option to sign-in automatically on next usage session. This is especially important on a mobile device where data input is more difficult than on a desktop.
>
> Note that if automatic sign-in is enabled, a sign-out link should also be provided.

3.3.2.2 How to do it

User credentials can be stored in a cookie or in local storage. However, it is important not to store unencrypted password information since this is insecure. Typically, a securely hashed token which, if necessary, can be revoked on the server, is stored locally in order to enable automatic sign-in.

Caching with a timestamp

Most web services allow you to hit their service a limited number of times per day. By using `localStorage` with a timestamp, you can cache results of web services locally and access them only after a specified time to refresh the data.

A simple library that allows for this memcache-like behavior is lscache (*https://github.com/pamelafox/lscache*). lscache emulates memcache functions using HTML5 `localStorage`, so that you can cache data on the client and associate an expiration time with each piece of data. If the `localStorage` limit (about 5MB) is exceeded, it tries to create space by removing the items that are closest to expiring anyway. If `localStorage` is not available at all in the browser, the library degrades by simply not caching, and all cache requests return null.

Syncing Data from the Client Side

All of the ways for Web Storage to speed up your web application discussed so far, are forms of one-way communication for which syncing, or transmitting modified JSON objects, back to the server is not required. Instead, you simply push data to the browser and use it as a cache.

Today, companies are just starting to leverage Web Storage to store and sync the object model back to the server-side database. Such functionality is useful to:

- Allow a web app to function offline, then sync new client data to server
- Allow a web app to function offline, then refresh client data on reconnect
- Allow an offline web app and online server data to be changed, and then sync both datasets while handling conflicts

Some of these data management and versioning situations can get fairly complex. For example, LinkedIn recently posted its solution to managing RESTful JSON data with `localStorage`. The company's main reasoning for bringing `localStorage` into the picture was to reduce latency and unneeded network requests on its latest iPad app. According to LinkedIn engineer Akhilesh Gupta:

LinkedIn just released a brand new iPad app built using HTML5, *backbone.js*, and *under score.js*. The app includes a rich stream of information, which is a combination of network updates, group posts, and news articles. The user can also switch to specific streams like Co-Worker updates or news articles from a specific category.

For the full article, see *http://engineering.linkedin.com/mobile/linkedin-ipad-using-local-storage-snappy-mobile-apps*.

At its core, this particular application uses Backbone to manage client-side data models. The developers then wrote the necessary code to override the basic sync functionality to allow models and collections to be stored in `localStorage`. Again, this is clearly a performance move and doesn't really address syncing data back to the server. But, it is a more complex use case that manages versioning and migration of the data to newer versions of the app. In the end, the iPad application gained the following performance improvements:

- A more responsive application thanks to temporarily storing recently fetched data; users no longer have to wait for network requests to finish before moving around the application

- Seamless sharing of fetched data among multiple web views in the native application

- Independence from memory constraints in mobile devices; `localStorage` can store and populate temporary objects in memory when necessary

- Decreased memory footprint and rendering time while scrolling because complicated HTML document fragments are stored in `localStorage`

Database Syncing with Backbone

A few frameworks allow for data to be synced from `localStorage` back to the server. For example, *Backbone.js* comes with methods for fetching and saving data models to and from the server. Out of the box, however, it does not provide the advanced functionality required by an application that needs to work offline and synchronize with the server when online. To address this, Neil Bevis of the Dev Camp blog posted an excellent solution that I'll summarize here. (For the complete blog post, see *http://occdev camp.wordpress.com/2011/10/15/backbone-local-storage-and-server-synchronization*.)

Backbone-localstorage.js provides communication with `localStorage` by simply adding the JavaScript file to the project. By adding this file, however, you then cannot communicate between Backbone and the server with `Backbone.sync`. The first thing you must do is create a copy of the `Backbone.sync` method before it's replaced by the inclusion of the *backbone-localstorage.js* JavaScript file:

```
<script src="backbone.js"></script>
<script>Backbone.serverSync = Backbone.sync;</script>
<script src="backbone-localstorage.js"></script>
```

Now, you'll be able to save data to the server using:

```
Backbone.serverSync('update', model, options);
```

This gives the standard model.fetch() and model.save() functions the ability to use localStorage. Next, you must provide a synchronized flag with a Boolean value describing its client-side status. When the client is ready to push local changes to the server from a given collection, it sends model objects with synchronized=false on a model-by-model basis using:

```
Backbone.serverSync('update', model, { success: 'foo', error: 'bar'}).
```

If the server responds with a different ID than what is stored on the client, then that means you have a new object. If the IDs remain the same, however, then you simply have an update. When a new object comes from the server, the following code deletes the existing ID in localStorage and adds the new version:

```
for (var i = 0; i < models.length; i++) {
    var model = models[i];
    if (model.get('synchronized')) { continue; }
    model.change();
    Backbone.serverSync('update', model, {
        success: function (data) {
            var model = collection.get(data.ClientId);
            //if new server will return a different Id
            if (data.ServerId != data.ClientId) {
                //delete from localStorage with current Id
                Backbone.sync("delete", model,
                    { success: function () { },
                      error: function () { } });

                //save model back into localStorage
                model.save({ Id: data.ServerId })
            }
            model.save({ synchronized: true });
            collection.localCacheActive = false;
        },
        error: function (jqTHX, textStatus, errorThrown) {
            console.log('Model upload failure:' + textStatus);
            collection.localCacheActive = false;
        }
    });
}
```

When asked to pull server-side changes to a collection from the server, the client first uses model.save() to save any unpushed client-side changes into localStorage. It next requests the entire collection from the server via the standard Backbone fetch method:

```
tempCollection.sync = Backbone.serverSync;
tempCollection.fetch( { success: blah, error: blah });
```

In practice, you could reduce the associated data download to only items that require updating. As it receives each model back from the server, the `success` function checks each one against its own list. If the model is new, `success` adds it to the collection that is updating and also uses `model.save()` to record it into local storage:

```
collection.add(tempModel);
tempModel.change();
tempModel.save({ synchronized: true });
```

Finally, the `success` function updates the model with revised data after the model has been synchronized:

```
model.set(tempModel.toJSON());
model.set({ synchronized: true });
model.save();
```

The big issue with this approach is if the model already exists and the user has made `localStorage`-based modifications to it. In this code, those models are not updated during the pull of server-side changes. Those objects are pushed to the server to be updated in the database.

This is not an end-all solution, and there are many frameworks currently trying to address this problem. Many of the solutions are just as mature as the one reviewed here. So your use of `localStorage` and syncing to a server-side database will be dictated by the complexity of your use case.

Using Web Storage in Any Browser

Although you can use `localStorage` safely within most modern web browsers, if your application must accommodate browsers without `localStorage`, you can use some easy-to-follow, lightweight polyfills. For example, the following example polyfill accommodates IE 6 and 7, as well as Firefox 2 and 3. With the exact same API as defined in the Web Storage spec, you can start using it today with roughly 90 lines of JavaScript included in your application. (For the full source, see *https://raw.github.com/wojodesign/local-storage-js/master/storage.js*.)

```
(function(){
    var window = this;
    // check to see if we have localStorage or not
    if( !window.localStorage ){

        // globalStorage
        // non-standard: Firefox 2+
        // https://developer.mozilla.org/en/dom/storage#globalStorage
        if ( window.globalStorage ) {
            // try/catch for file protocol in Firefox
            try {
                window.localStorage = window.globalStorage;
            } catch( e ) {}
```

```
        return;
}

// userData
// non-standard: IE 5+
// http://msdn.microsoft.com/en-us/library/ms531424(v=vs.85).aspx
var div = document.createElement( "div" ),
    attrKey = "localStorage";
div.style.display = "none";
document.getElementsByTagName( "head" )[ 0 ].appendChild( div );
if ( div.addBehavior ) {
    div.addBehavior( "#default#userdata" );

    var localStorage = window["localStorage"] = {
        "length":0,
        "setItem":function( key , value ){
            div.load( attrKey );
            key = cleanKey(key );

            if( !div.getAttribute( key ) ){
                this.length++;
            }
            div.setAttribute( key , value );

            div.save( attrKey );
        },
        "getItem":function( key ){
            div.load( attrKey );
            key = cleanKey(key );
            return div.getAttribute( key );

        },
        "removeItem":function( key ){
            div.load( attrKey );
            key = cleanKey(key );
            div.removeAttribute( key );

            div.save( attrKey );
            this.length--;
            if( this.length < 0 ){
                this.length=0;
            }
        },

        "clear":function(){
            div.load( attrKey );
            var i = 0;
            while ( attr =
            div.XMLDocument.documentElement.attributes[ i++ ] ) {
                div.removeAttribute( attr.name );
            }
            div.save( attrKey );
```

```
        this.length=0;
    },

    "key":function( key ){
        div.load( attrKey );
        return
        div.XMLDocument.documentElement.attributes[ key ];
    }

},

// convert invalid characters to dashes
// http://www.w3.org/TR/REC-xml/#NT-Name
// simplified to assume the starting character is valid
cleanKey = function( key ){
    return key.replace( /[^-._0-9A-Za-z\xb7\xc0-\xd6\xd8-\xf6\xf8-\u037d\u37f-\
                         u1fff\u200c-\u200d\u203f\u2040\u2070-\u218f]/g, "-" );
};


div.load( attrKey );
localStorage["length"] =
div.XMLDocument.documentElement.attributes.length;
    }
  }
})();
```

Frameworks

A few JavaScript frameworks address Web Storage needs on mobile devices. When evaluating Web Storage frameworks, look for a nice consistent storage API that works across all devices. Of course, this is what the spec itself does through a simple JavaScript API, but until all devices support this specification, you need a helper framework.

LawnChair

LawnChair (*http://westcoastlogic.com/lawnchair*) is designed with mobile in mind. Supporting all major mobile browsers, it's adaptive to the mobile and desktop environments described in this book and gives you a consistent API for accessing some form of lo calStorage. LawnChair allows you to store and query data on browsers without worrying about the underlying API. It's also agnostic to any server-side implementations, enabling you to get started quickly with a simple, lightweight framework.

The page setup is:

```
<!DOCTYPE html>
<html>
<head>
    <title>my app</theitle>
</head>
```

```
<body>
    <script src="lawnchair.js"></script>
</body>
</html>
```

To persist data, use:

```
Lawnchair(function(){
    this.save({msg:'hooray!'})
})
```

persistence.js

Supporting all major mobile browser platforms, *persistence.js* (*http://persistencejs.org*) is an asynchronous JavaScript object-relational mapper. It integrates with *Node.js* and server-side MySQL databases and is recommended for server-side use, because using in-memory data storage seems to slow down filtering and sorting. The download size is much heavier than that of LawnChair.

For page setup, use:

```
<!DOCTYPE html>
<html>
<head>
    <title>my app</title>
</head>
<body>
    <script src="persistence.js" type="application/javascript"></script>
<script src="persistence.store.sql.js" type="application/javascript"></script>
<script src="persistence.store.websql.js" type="application/javascript"></script>
</body>
</html>

if (window.openDatabase) {
    persistence.store.websql.config(persistence, "jquerymobile", 'database',
                                                        5 * 1024 * 1024);
} else {
    persistence.store.memory.config(persistence);
}

  persistence.define('Order', {
    shipping: "TEXT"
  });

  persistence.schemaSync();
```

Similar to Hibernate (JBoss's persistence framework), *persistence.js* uses a tracking mechanism to determine which objects changes have to be persisted to the database. All objects retrieved from the database are automatically tracked for changes. New entities can be tracked and persisted using the `persistence.add` function:

```
var c = new Category({name: "Main category"});
persistence.add(c);
```

All changes made to tracked objects can be flushed to the database by using `persistence.flush`, which takes a transaction object and callback function as arguments. You can start a new transaction using `persistence.transaction`:

```
persistence.transaction(function(tx) {
  persistence.flush(tx, function() {
    alert('Done flushing!');
  });
});
```

CHAPTER 7
Geolocation

The Geolocation API provides scripted access to geographical location information associated with the hosting device. This gives your applications the ability to locate users and track their latitude and longitude as they move about. This functionality could be used for many interesting use cases such as:

Geofencing
> Give your app the ability to schedule a task to alert users the moment they enter or leave a location. You could also target ads for users within a certain city or state.

Geocoding
> Combine your app with a service like the Google Maps API (Figure 7-1), and you can translate latitude and longitude coordinates into actual postal addresses.

General tracking
> Track distances driven, walked, or ran.

The API itself is device agnostic; it doesn't care how the browser determines location. The underlying mechanism to obtain the user's actual location may be through WiFi, GPS, or by the user actually entering a zip code into the device. The API is designed to gather both "one-shot" position requests and repeated position updates. Of course, Geolocation is no different than any of the other HTML5e APIs in regard to bugs, workarounds, and differences in implementations across browsers. After a review of the basics, we'll dive into the cross-browser nuances.

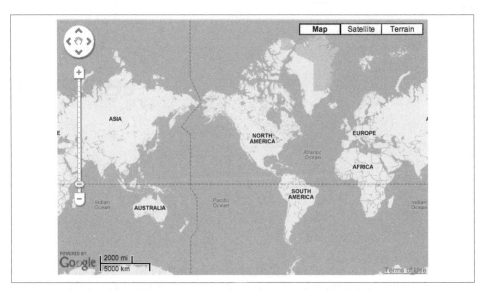

Figure 7-1. Using the Google Maps API with Geolocation

To access a user's location, run the following JavaScript:

```
navigator.geolocation.getCurrentPosition(function(){//show a map});
```

The web browser asks the user for permission to reveal his location, as shown in Figure 7-2.

Figure 7-2. User alert when accessing Geolocation

After receiving permission, the browser returns a `position` object with a `coords` attribute. This allows you to call the following properties, from which you can learn the user's latitude, longitude, and many other data points:

```
position.coords.latitude //geographic coordinate in decimal degrees
position.coords.longitude //geographic coordinate in decimal degrees
position.coords.altitude //the height of the position (meters above the ellipsoid)
```

```
position.coords.accuracy //accuracy level of latitude and longitude coordinates
position.coords.altitudeAccuracy //specified in meters
position.coords.heading // direction of travel of the hosting device in degrees
position.coords.speed //the device's current velocity (meters per second)
```

Only the `latitude`, `longitude`, and `accuracy` properties are guaranteed to be available. The rest might come back null, depending on the capabilities of the user's device and the backend positioning server that it talks to.

The `getCurrentPosition()` function has an optional third argument, a `PositionOp tions` object:

```
navigator.geolocation.getCurrentPosition(successCallback,errorCallback,
    { enableHighAccuracy: true, timeout: 10000, maximumAge: 6000 });
```

The `enableHighAccuracy` attribute provides a hint that the application would like to receive the best possible results. If this attribute is true, the device can support it, and the user consents, then the device will try to provide an exact location. Using this attribute may result in slower response times or increased power consumption. The user might also deny this capability, or the device might have more accurate results to provide. The intended purpose of this attribute is to allow applications to inform the implementation that they do not require high accuracy Geolocation fixes and, therefore, the implementation can avoid using Geolocation providers that consume a significant amount of power (think GPS).

The `timeout` property is the number of milliseconds your web application is willing to wait for a position. This timer doesn't start counting down until after the user gives permission to share position data. You're not timing the user; you're timing the network.

The `maximumAge` attribute indicates that the application is willing to accept a cached position whose age is no greater than the specified time in milliseconds. This gives you a window of time to pull a cached location from the user device. By defining this attribute, you are saying that you're fine with where this device was located at x milliseconds in the past.

Your web app will dictate exactly the specificity of your Geolocation needs. So keep in mind battery life and latencies on the user device when you use the above properties. If you need to track the location of the user continuously, the spec defines the `watchPosi tion()` function. It has the same structure as `getCurrentPosition()` and will call the `successCallback` whenever the device position changes:

```
navigator.geolocation.watchPosition(successCallback,errorCallback,
    { enableHighAccuracy: true, timeout: 10000, maximumAge: 6000 });
```

Use watchPosition() with care in Mobile Safari running on iOS5. As of this writing, there is a known issue: the page will run for roughly four minutes, after which the user will receive a "JavaScript execution exceeded timeout" error. To work around the watch Position() issue on iOS5, you can implement the following code using getCurrentPo sition() with setInterval():

```
var geolocationID;
(function getLocation() {
    var count = 0;
    geolocationID = window.setInterval(
      function () {
          count++;
          if (count > 3) {  //when count reaches a number, reset interval
              window.clearInterval(geolocationID);
              getLocation();
          } else {
              navigator.
              geolocation.getCurrentPosition(successCallback, errorCallback,
                { enableHighAccuracy: true, timeout: 10000 });
          }
      },
      600000); //end setInterval;
})();
```

Another issue with the specific WebKit Geolocation implementation, is that accessing geolocation activates the Geolocation service, which currently blocks page caching (*https://bugs.webkit.org/show_bug.cgi?id=43956*). If you simply check the geolocation property, you can avoid this issue:

```
function supports_geolocation() {
   try {
     return 'geolocation' in navigator &&
     navigator['geolocation'] !== null;
   } catch (e) {
     return false;
   }
}
```

You can view a live demo with all implemented workarounds at *http://html5e.org/exam ple/geo*.

A Practical Use Case: User Tracking

To track a user over a set of latitude and longitude coordinates, you can use the Haversine formula. With it, your application can calculate the shortest distance over the Earth's surface and provide an as-the-crow-flies distance between the points. The code you need is:

```
function calculateDistance(lat1, lon1, lat2, lon2) {
   var R = 6371; // km
```

```
    var dLat = (lat2 - lat1).toRad();
    var dLon = (lon2 - lon1).toRad();
    var a = Math.sin(dLat / 2) * Math.sin(dLat / 2) +
            Math.cos(lat1.toRad()) * Math.cos(lat2.toRad()) *
            Math.sin(dLon / 2) * Math.sin(dLon / 2);
    var c = 2 * Math.atan2(Math.sqrt(a), Math.sqrt(1 - a));
    var d = R * c;
    return d;
}
Number.prototype.toRad = function() {
    return this * Math.PI / 180;
}
```

This distance calculation, along with many others, is available at *http://www.movable-type.co.uk/scripts/latlong.html* under the Creative Commons Attribution 3.0 License.

A Practical Use Case: Reverse Geocoding

The term "geocoding" generally refers to translating a human-readable address into a location on a map. The process of doing the converse, translating a location on the map into a human-readable address, is known as *reverse geocoding*. The following code is a simple example of how to reverse geocode coordinates returned from the Geolocation API with the Google Maps API:

```
<!DOCTYPE html>
<html>
  <head>
    <meta name="viewport" content="initial-scale=1.0, user-scalable=no">
    <meta charset="utf-8">
    <title>
Google Maps JavaScript API v3 Example: Reverse Geocoding
</title>
    <link
href="https://google-developers.appspot.com/maps/documentation/
                                javascript/examples/default.css"
rel="stylesheet">
    <script
src="https://maps.googleapis.com/maps/api/js?sensor=false">
</script>
    <script>
      var geocoder;
      var map;
      var infowindow = new google.maps.InfoWindow();
      var marker;
      function initialize() {
        geocoder = new google.maps.Geocoder();
        var latlng = new google.maps.LatLng(40.730885,-73.997383);
        var mapOptions = {
          zoom: 8,
          center: latlng,
          mapTypeId: 'roadmap'
```

```
      }
      map = new google.
      maps.Map(document.getElementById('map_canvas'), mapOptions);
    }

    function codeLatLng() {
      var input = document.getElementById('latlng').value;
      var latlngStr = input.split(',', 2);
      var lat = parseFloat(latlngStr[0]);
      var lng = parseFloat(latlngStr[1]);
      var latlng = new google.maps.LatLng(lat, lng);
      geocoder.geocode({'latLng': latlng}, function(results, status) {
        if (status == google.maps.GeocoderStatus.OK) {
          if (results[1]) {
            map.setZoom(11);
            marker = new google.maps.Marker({
                position: latlng,
                map: map
            });
            infowindow.setContent(results[1].formatted_address);
            infowindow.open(map, marker);
          } else {
            alert('No results found');
          }
        } else {
          alert('Geocoder failed due to: ' + status);
        }
      });
    }
  </script>
</head>
<body onload="initialize()">
  <div>
    <input id="latlng" type="textbox" value="40.714224,-73.961452">
  </div>
  <div>
    <input type="button" value="Reverse Geocode" onclick="codeLatLng()">
  </div>
  <div id="map_canvas"
  style="height: 90%; top:60px; border: 1px solid black;"></div>
</body>
</html>
```

Frameworks

When working with the Geolocation API, you should detect and wrap available Geolocation mechanisms that are available across different mobile devices. For example,

you could detect Google Gears, BlackBerry, and the default Geolocation API within one JavaScript `init()` method. But why try to code all this yourself, when you could just use a framework? The Geolocation JavaScript frameworks are relatively small in both size and selection.

geo-location-javascript

A mobile centric framework using nonstandard BlackBerry and WebOD tricks, geo-location-javascript (*http://code.google.com/p/geo-location-javascript*) wraps the underlying platform-specific implementation through a simple JavaScript API that is aligned to the W3C Geolocation API specification. Under an MIT license, geo-location-javascript supports a range of platforms, including iOS, Android, Black-Berry OS, browsers with Google Gears support (Android, Windows Mobile), Nokia Web Run-Time (Nokia N97), webOS Application Platform (Palm Pre), Torch Mobile Iris Browser, and Mozilla Geode.

To setup and use the API, the code you need is:

```
<html>
<head>
        <title>Javascript geo sample</title>
        <script src="http://code.google.com/apis/gears/gears_init.js"
                type="text/javascript" charset="utf-8"></script>
        <script
            src="js/geo.js" type="text/javascript"
            charset="utf-8"></script>
</head>
<body>
        <b>Javascript geo sample</b>
        <script>
                if(geo_position_js.init()){
                        geo_position_js.getCurrentPosition(success_callback,
                        error_callback,
{enableHighAccuracy:true});
                }
                else{
                        alert("Functionality not available");
                }

                function success_callback(p)
                {
                        alert('lat='+p.coords.latitude.toFixed(2)+';
                        lon='+p.coords.longitude.toFixed(2));
                }

                function error_callback(p)
                {
                        alert('error='+p.message);
```

```
        }
    </script>
    </body>
</html>
```

Webshims lib

Supporting all jQuery's A-graded browsers and the latest Opera, the Webshims (*http://afarkas.github.com/webshim/demos*) framework is based on jQuery and Modernizr and falls under an MIT license. It tries to handle many different polyfills and shims, including Gelocation.

The set-up and usage code looks like this:

```
<!DOCTYPE html>
<html lang="en">
<head>
    <script
    src="http://ajax.googleapis.com/ajax/libs/jquery/1.7.1/jquery.min.js">
    </script>
    <script src="../js-webshim/minified/extras/modernizr-custom.js"></script>
    <script src="../js-webshim/minified/polyfiller.js"></script>
    <script>
        $.webshims.setOptions('geolocation', {
            confirmText: '{location} wants to know your position. It is Ok.'
        });
        //load all polyfill features
        //or load only a specific feature with $.webshims.polyfill('feature-name');
        $.webshims.polyfill();
    </script>
```

A few other scripts try to handle this polyfill, including:

- Geolocation API crossbrowser support (*http://bit.ly/Geolocation-API-Polyfill*)
- HTML5 Geolocation with fallback (*http://gist.github.com/366184*)

Currently, one of the greatest drawbacks to using the Geolocation API within a mobile web browser is not having the ability to run in the background after the browser has closed. For example, it gets extremely difficult to track the user in the background and allow the person to switch to another app outside of the mobile browser. At this point, your browser must remain open as a background process for your Geolocation-based app to work properly.

## CHAPTER 8

Device Orientation API

Accelerometers, gyroscopes, and compasses are now commonplace in mobile devices and laptops. With the Device Orientation API, you can capture movements at an extremely fine-grained level, receiving exact details on the motion and acceleration of the device.

Conceptually, an accelerometer behaves as a damped mass on a spring. When the accelerometer experiences an acceleration, the mass is displaced to the point that the spring is able to accelerate the mass at the same rate as the casing. The displacement is then measured to give the acceleration.

With applications ranging from military-based inertial guidance systems to tracking animals to measuring earthquakes and aftershocks, orientation hardware has been in use for quite some time. Now you have the opportunity to add this functionality to your applications to enhance how devices are tracked and interact with your user interface. It's time to move beyond using the Device Orientation API only for games and simple Geolocation.

To begin, you need to understand the basics of the API and handling the measurements in JavaScript. The first DOM event provided by the specification, `deviceorientation`, supplies the physical orientation of the device, expressed as a series of rotations from a local coordinate frame. Here's a simple check to see if this browser supports the `DeviceOrientationEvent` object:

```
supports_orientation : function() {
  try {
  return 'DeviceOrientationEvent' in
  window && window['DeviceOrientationEvent'] !== null
  } catch (e) {
  return false;
  }
}
```

Next, you must add an event listener to listen for changes in the device orientation:

```
if (window.DeviceOrientationEvent) {
    window.addEventListener("deviceorientation", function( event ) {
    //alpha: rotation around z-axis
    var rotateDegrees = event.alpha;
    //gamma: left to right
    var leftToRight = event.gamma;
    //beta: front back motion
    var frontToBack = event.beta;

    handleOrientationEvent( frontToBack, leftToRight, rotateDegrees );
    }, false);
}

var handleOrientationEvent =
    function( frontToBack, leftToRight, rotateDegrees ){
    //do something with the event
};
```

Now that you have the data, what do the variables mean and how do you put them to use? When you tilt the device from side to side, this is referred to as *beta* (Figure 8-1). Tilting from front to back is *gamma* (Figure 8-2), and rotating the phone while facing up (on the Z axis) is known as *alpha* (Figure 8-3).

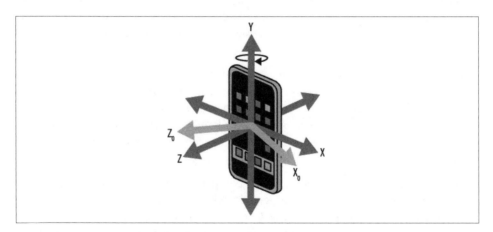

Figure 8-1. Beta positioning for the Device Orientation API

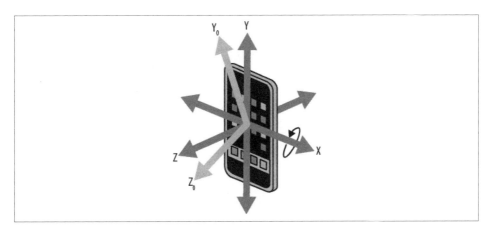

Figure 8-2. Gamma positioning for the Device Orientation API

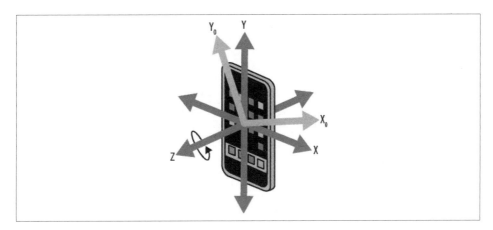

Figure 8-3. Alpha positioning Device Orientation API

One browser-related caveat to remember: older versions of Firefox (3.6, 4, and 5) supported `mozOrientation` versus the standard `DeviceOrientation` event. You must normalize the data to radians if you want to match what is currently provided by the newer specification. Here's how:

```
if (!evt.gamma && !evt.beta) {
    //If this is Firefox 3.6, 4, or 5, convert
    // the degree data to radians
    evt.gamma = -(evt.x * (180 / Math.PI));
    evt.beta = -(evt.y * (180 / Math.PI));
}
```

A Practical Use Case: Scrolling with Device Movement

The typical business use for the Device Orientation API is to couple orientation hardware with Geolocation to enhance the user's actual position and direction on a given map. But, what if you could tilt your device left or right to navigate through pages? A flick of the wrist gets you to the next page. Or, you could deliver a continuous scrolling slideshow based on left or right movement. I think you get the point, now let's code it.

If you combine the transition code for sliding from one page to another in Chapter 3 with the Device Orientation API, you can create a slideshow of pages that navigate based on which direction the device is tilted. You can find a demo of this in action at *http://html5e.org/example/orientation*.

First, set up your CSS transforms for left and right movement:

```
var handleOrientationEvent = function (frontToBack, leftToRight, rotateDegrees) {
  //on each movement, we're controlling how the current focusPage moves
  var curTransform =
      new window.WebKitCSSMatrix(window.
      getComputedStyle(focusPage).webkitTransform);
  focusPage.innerHTML = leftToRight;
  focusPage.style.webkitTransform =
  'translate3d(' + leftToRight * 5 + 'px, 0, 0)';
  focusPage.style.WebkitTransition = 'all .5s ease-out';
  navigate(leftToRight);
};
```

Next, perform the navigation on all the defined pages in the DOM with the single page model from Chapter 3:

```
var keepgoing = true, pagehistory = [];

var pagestate = function(pages, className) {
  var that = {};
  that.count = 0;
  that.pages = pages;
  that.pageCount = pages.length;
  that.className = className;
  return that;
};

var allpages = listToArray(document.querySelectorAll('.page'));

var leftPageState = new pagestate(allpages, 'page stage-left');
var rightPageState = new pagestate(allpages.slice(), 'page stage-right');

function detecttilt(leftToRight) {
  if (keepgoing) {
    if (leftToRight > 30) {
      donav(leftPageState, rightPageState);
    } else if (leftToRight < -30) {
```

```
      donav(rightPageState, leftPageState);
    }
  }
}

function donav(ps, ops) {
  var page;
  if (ps.count <= (ps.pageCount + 1)) {
    //reset
    if (ps.count === 0) {
      if (pagehistory.length > 0) {
        ps.pages = pagehistory;
        pagehistory = [];
      }
      ps.count++;
    } else {
      page = ps.pages.pop();
      if (page !== undefined) {
        page.className = ps.className;
        pagehistory.push(page);
        ps.count++;
        console.log(ps.count);
        slideQueue(page);
      } else {
        ops.count = 0;
      }
    }
  }
}

function slideQueue(page) {
  keepgoing = false;
  // A simple way to put a block on the calling code, because
  // the orientation is a constant change
  slidfast.ui.slideTo(page, function () {
    keepgoing = true;
  });
}
```

This demo has been tested on WebKit-based devices such as Safari, Android, and Chrome. Even better, because you are using the same CSS transitions from Chapter 3, it should work on Firefox and Opera Mobile browsers as well.

## CHAPTER 9

Web Workers

When your web application requires heavy lifting or background processing on the JavaScript side, the Web Workers API is your answer.

The Web Workers interface spawns real OS-level threads, allowing for data to be passed back and forth between any given threads (or worker). Furthermore, because communication points between threads are carefully controlled, concurrency problems are rare. You cannot access components unsafe to threads or the DOM, and you have to pass specific data in and out of a thread through serialized objects. So you have to work extremely hard to cause problems in your code. Regardless of how you plan to use Web Workers in your application, the main idea behind processing any behind-the-scenes data lies in the idea of creating multiple workers (or threads) in the browser.

As of this writing, Safari, Safari for iOS5, Chrome, Opera, and Mozilla Firefox support the Web Workers API, but Internet Explorer does not. (Internet Explorer 10 did add support for Web Workers in Platform Preview 2.) Web Workers in Android versions 2.0 and 2.1 support Web Workers, as well, but later versions of Android do not. The only shim currently available for Web Workers makes use of Google Gears. If the core Web Workers API is not supported on a device or browser, you can detect if Google Gears is installed. For more details, see *http://html5-shims.googlecode.com/svn/trunk/demo/work ers.html*.

With Web Workers and its multithreaded approach, you do not have access to the DOM (which is not thread safe), the `window`, `document`, or `parent` objects. You do, however, have access to the quite a few other features and objects, starting with the `navigator` object:

```
appCodeName     //the code name of the browser
appName     //the name of the browser
```

```
appVersion      //the version information of the browser
cookieEnabled      //Determines whether cookies are enabled in the browser
platform      //Returns for which platform the browser is compiled
userAgent      //the user-agent header sent by the browser to the server
```

Although you can access the `location` object, it is read only:

```
hash      //the anchor portion of a URL
host      //the hostname and port of a URL
hostname      //the hostname of a URL
href      //the entire URL
pathname      //the path name of a URL
port      //the port number the server uses for a URL
protocol      //the protocol of a URL
search      //the query portion of a URL
```

You can use `XMLHttpRequest` to make AJAX calls within a worker, as well as import external scripts using the `importScripts()` method, as long as they're in the same domain. To cut down wait times, you can set and clear timeouts and intervals with `setTimeout()`, `clearTimeout()`, `setInterval()`, and `clearInterval()`, respectively. Finally, you can access the Application cache and spawn other workers. Creating a worker is quite easy; you need only a JavaScript file's URL. The `Worker()` constructor is invoked with the URL to that file as its only argument:

```
var worker = new Worker('worker.js');
```

 Worker scripts must be external files with the same scheme as their calling page. Thus, you cannot load a script from a data URL and an HTTPS page cannot start worker scripts that begin with HTTP URLs.

The worker is not actually started until you call `postMessage()`, such as by sending some object data to the worker:

```
worker.postMessage({'haz':'foo'}); // Start the worker.
```

Next, add an `EventListener` to listen for data the worker returns:

```
worker.addEventListener('message', function(e) {
  console.log('returned data from worker', e.data);
}, false);
```

In the actual *worker.js* file, you could have something simple like:

```
self.addEventListener('message', function(e) {
  var data = e.data;
  //Manipulate data and send back to parent
  self.postMessage(data.haz); //posts 'foo' to parent DOM
}, false);
```

The previous example simply relays serialized JSON from the parent DOM to the spawned worker instance, and back again.

In newer browsers (like Chrome), you can take your data types a step further and pass binary data between workers. With transferable objects, data is transferred from one context to another. It is zero-copy, which vastly improves the performance of sending data to a worker.

When you transfer an `ArrayBuffer` from your main app to a worker, the original `ArrayBuffer` is cleared and is made no longer usable by the browser. Its contents are transferred to the worker context.

Chrome version 8 and above also includes a new version of `postMessage()` that supports transferable objects:

```
var uInt8Array = new Uint8Array(new ArrayBuffer(10));
for (var i = 0; i < uInt8Array.length; ++i) {
  uInt8Array[i] = i * 2; // [0, 2, 4, 6, 8,...]
}

worker.webkitPostMessage(uInt8View.buffer, [uInt8View.buffer]);
```

Figure 9-1 shows how much faster data can travel between threads using transferable objects. For example, 32MB of data makes a round trip from the worker back to the parent in 2ms. Using previous methods, such as structured cloning, took upward of 300ms to copy the data between threads. To try this test for yourself, visit *http://html5-demos.appspot.com/static/workers/transferables/index.html*.

```
Run test

07:48:50:541 thread: USING TRANSFERABLE OBJECTS :)
07:48:50:543 thread: READY!
07:48:51:026 worker: READY! [07:48:51:024]
07:48:56:587 thread: filled 32 MB buffer
07:48:56:589 thread: postMessage roundtrip took: 2 ms
07:48:56:589 thread: postMessage roundtrip rate: 16000 MB/s
```

Figure 9-1. Using Web Workers with transferable objects

A Practical Use Case: Pooling and Parallelizing Jobs

The following example, originally inspired by Jos Dirksen's thread pool example, gives you a way to specify the number of concurrent workers (or threads). With this method, browsers like Chrome can use multiple CPU cores when processing data concurrently, and you can significantly increase your rendering time by up to 300%. You can view the full demo here at *http://html5e.org/example/workers*, but the basic *worker1.js* file contains:

```
self.onmessage = function(event) {

    var myobj = event.data;
```

```
    search: while (myobj.foo < 200) {
        myobj.foo += 1;
        for (var i = 2; i <= Math.sqrt(myobj.foo); i += 1)
            if (myobj.foo % i == 0)
                continue search;
        // found a prime!
        self.postMessage(myobj);
    }

    // close this worker
    self.close();
};
```

The above code simply spits out prime numbers and ends at 200. You could set the `while` loop to `while(true)` for endless output of prime numbers, but this is a simple example to demonstrate how you can process data in chunks and parallelize the code to reach a common goal with multiple worker threads.

From your main *index.html* (the place you want all the data to be displayed), initialize your thread pool and give the workers a callback:

```
slidfast({
    workers: {script:'worker1.js', threads:9, mycallback:workerCallback}
});
```

 To view a live demo of this technique, visit *https://github.com/html5e/ slidfast/blob/master/example/workers/index.html*.

When the `workers` parameter initializes, the following code creates the thread pool and begins each task concurrently:

```
function Pool(size) {
  var _this = this;

  // set some defaults
  this.taskQueue = [];
  this.workerQueue = [];
  this.poolSize = size;

  this.addWorkerTask = function (workerTask) {
      if (_this.workerQueue.length > 0) {
          // get the worker from the front of the queue
          var workerThread = _this.workerQueue.shift();
          //get an index for tracking
          slidfast.worker.obj().index = _this.workerQueue.length;
          workerThread.run(workerTask);
      } else {
          // no free workers,
```

```
            _this.taskQueue.push(workerTask);
        }
    };

    this.init = function () {
        // create 'size' number of worker threads
        for (var i = 0; i < size; i++) {
            _this.workerQueue.push(new WorkerThread(_this));
        }
    };

    this.freeWorkerThread = function (workerThread) {
        if (_this.taskQueue.length > 0) {
            // don't put back in queue, but execute next task
            var workerTask = _this.taskQueue.shift();
            workerThread.run(workerTask);
        } else {
            _this.taskQueue.push(workerThread);
        }
    };
}

// runner work tasks in the pool
function WorkerThread(parentPool) {

    var _this = this;

    this.parentPool = parentPool;
    this.workerTask = {};

    this.run = function (workerTask) {
        this.workerTask = workerTask;
        // create a new web worker
        if (this.workerTask.script !== null) {
            var worker = new Worker(workerTask.script);
            worker.addEventListener('message', function (event) {
                mycallback(event);
                _this.parentPool.freeWorkerThread(_this);
            }, false);
            worker.postMessage(slidfast.worker.obj());
        }
    };

}

function WorkerTask(script, callback, msg) {
    this.script = script;
    this.callback = callback;
    console.log(msg);
    this.obj = msg;
}
```

```
var pool = new Pool(workers.threads);
pool.init();
var workerTask = new WorkerTask(workers.script,
                                mycallback,
                                slidfast.worker.obj());
```

After initializing the worker threads, add the actual workerTasks to process the data:

```
pool.addWorkerTask(workerTask);
slidfast.worker.obj().foo = 10;
pool.addWorkerTask(workerTask);
slidfast.worker.obj().foo = 20;
pool.addWorkerTask(workerTask);
slidfast.worker.obj().foo = 30;
pool.addWorkerTask(workerTask);
```

As you can see in Figure 9-2, each thread brings data back to the main page and renders it with the supplied callback. The thread order varies on each refresh and there is no guarantee on how the browser will process the data. To see a demo, visit *http:// html5e.org/example/workers*. Use the latest version of Chrome or another browser that supports actual CPU core usage per web worker.

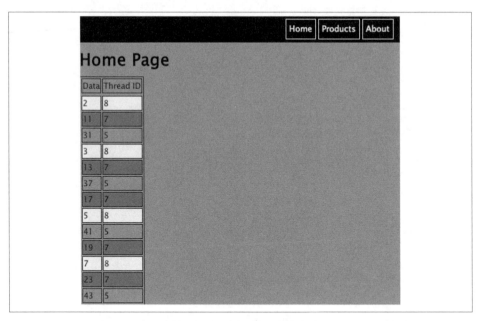

Figure 9-2. Data being returned by multiple Web Worker threads in parallel

Other Uses

Crunching prime numbers may not be the best real-world example of using thread pooling, but you can use the same technique for processing image data. For more information, see *http://www.smartjava.org/examples/webworkers2* and Figure 9-3.

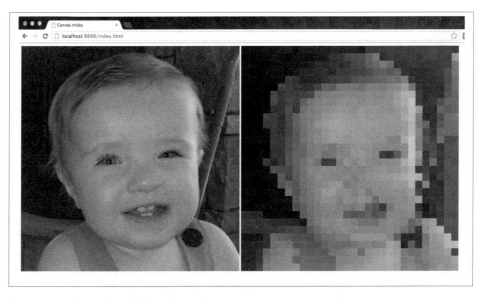

Figure 9-3. Example of Web Worker threads processing image data

Web Workers could be put into action within your app for additional scenarios as well. For example, you could parse wiki text as the user types, and then generate the HTML. You can find an example of this at *http://www.cach.me/blog/2011/01/javascript-web-workers-tutorial-parse-wiki-text-in-real-time*. Or, you could use it for visualizations and business graphs. For a visualization framework, see *https://github.com/samizdatco/arbor*.

Index

Symbols

100% JavaScript Driven approach, 52–59
   Sencha Touch, 52–54
   Wink Toolkit, 54–56

A

accelerometers, 137
Adobe Shadow (mobile debugger), 60
adoptNode, 41
AJAX calls
   security concerns with, 39
Ajax Minifier online CSS compressor (Microsoft), 77
Amber.js, 88
Android
   rendering rotating transition, 29
Android default browser, 10
   Dolphin browserr, 10
Angular framework
   Google, 89
   security features with, 90
   server synchronization, 89
Apache ActiveMQ, 96
Apache, HTTP compression support in, 74
Apple, 2
   and Ember framework, 88
approaches
   100% JavaScript Driven, 52–59

   no-page-structure approach, 51
   single page, 48–50
apps, 19 (see web apps)
asynchronous nonblocking IO (NIO), 96
Atmosphere (WebSocket framework), 108
automatic sign-in, implementing, 119

B

Backbone (client side MV* framework), 65
Backbone framework, 85–87, 121
   and legacy servers, 87
   server synchronization, 86
background-repeat CSS, 22
Batman framework (Shopify), 90
   server synchronization, 91
body onload event, 43
Boot 2 Gecko project (Mozilla), 4
Boot to Gecko project (B2G), 12
borders CSS, 22
box-shadow CSS, 22

C

caching, 37–41
   defined, 37
   and storage limitations, 39
   time stamps, adding, 120
Chrome, 114
   debugging web apps, as tool for, 33

We'd like to hear your suggestions for improving our indexes. Send email to index@oreilly.com.

geolocation, 129–136
  accessing through JavaScript, 130
  drawbacks, 136
  frameworks, 134
  reverse geocoding, 133
  user tracking, 132
Geolocation API, 15
geolocation API, 129–132
geolocation frameworks, 134
  geo-location-javascript, 135
  Webshims lib, 136
getCurrentPosition() (Geolocation API), 131
GlassFish application server, 98
Google, 2
  Web Storage, use of, 117
Google Gears, 135
Google Maps API, 133
gradient CSS, 22
grunt (minification tool), 78–82
Gupta, Akhilesh, 120
gyroscopes, 137
GZIP compression, 74–75

H

Hacker News, 5
HAProxy, 105
hardware acceleration, 21
  Android Froyo and, 24
  debugging, 31–34
  memory allocation/computational burden
    concerns, 22
  memory consumption, 36
  overlapping acceleration concerns, 22
  power consumption/battery life concerns, 22
  transforms, 2D vs. 3D, 24
hardware APIs, 15
Haversine formula, 132
HTML5
  enterprise development, 15
  and movement away from server-side archi-
    tecture, 2
  vs. JSON/XML, 64
HTML5 Enterprise (HTML5e) browsers, 15
HTML5Boilerplate.com, 75
HTTP compression (see compression (HTTP))

I

iframe
  vs. innerHTML(), 41
innerHTML()
  AJAX responses and, 37
  vs. iframe, 41
interactions/transitions, 23–36
  flipping, 27–29
  rotating, 29–30
  sliding, 23–25
Internet Explorer, 7
Internet Explorer Mobile, 13
interoperability
  and polyfills, 16
  translate3d(0,0,0), non-universal support for,
    24
  vendor prefix, 25
  and Web Storage, 123

J

Java, 3
Java EE 6.0 [Full Profile] application server, 98
JavaScript APIs
  and hardware access, 4
JavaScript frameworks, 46–59
  dangers of relying on, 46
  evaluating, 47
  Smalltalk MVC vs., 4
JavaScript MVC frameworks
  Angular (Google), 89
  Backbone, 85–87
  Batman (Shopify), 90
  Ember, 88–89
  Knockout, 92
  server-side architecture and, 83–94
JAWR (minification tool), 82
JBoss AS7 application server, 97
Jetty, 98
jQTouch, 49
jQuery Mobile, 48–49
JSMin (minification tool), 77

K

Kaazing Gateway, 96
Knockout (client side MV* framework), 65
Knockout framework, 92
  server synchronization, 92

L

Lecomte, Julien, 77
Leroux, Brian, 51
LinkedIn, 65, 120
localStorage, 111
long polling, 96
lscache, 120

M

maximumAge attribute (Geolocation API), 131
Media Capture API, 15
Microsoft, 2
minification, 77–82
    CompressorRater, 78
    grunt, 78–82
    JAWR, 82
    Ziproxy, 82
Mobile Design Pattern Gallery (Neil), 21
Mobile Safari (iOS6), 10
    BugReporter, limitations on, 10
    innerHTML() bug, 10
mobile web, 7–16
    browser interoperability, 7
    browsers, 9–14
    browsers, grading, 14
    building applications for, 19–62
    client-side APIs and, 15
    defined, 7
    device emulators, 16
    fragmentation, 8
    mobile first development, 8, 8
    native vs. Mobile Web models, 19–22
    testing, 16
mobile web browsers, 9–14
    Firefox (Mozilla), 11
    graceful degradation, 16
    grading, 14
    Internet Explorer Mobile, 13
    market shares, 13
    Opera Mobile, 13
    WebKit, 9
MobileESP framework, 71
MobileESP project, 69
Modernizr.js framework, 66
mod_deflate module (Apache), 74
Mozilla, 2
    Boot to Gecko project (B2G), 12
    WebAPI OS, 12

MVC patterns(Model-View-Controller), 83–94

N

Neil, Theresa, 21
Network Information API, 43–46
no-page-structure approach, 51
    xui, 51
node.js (WebSocket framework), 106

O

onclose (WebSocket listener), 97
100% JavaScript Driven approach
    The-M-Project, 57
onload event, 44
onmessage (WebSocket listener), 97
ononline event, 44
onopen (WebSocket listener), 97
opacity animation, 22
Open Web, 2
Opera
    private browsing, 117
Opera Dragonfly
    debugging web apps with, 61
Opera Mobile, 13
Orange Labs (France Telecom R&D), 54

P

Packer (minification tool), 77
performance
    CSS, issues with, 22
    and HTTP compression, 72
persistence.js framework, 126
PhoneGap framework, 51
Platform.js library, 70
polyfills, 16
Pretty Diff online CSS compressor, 77
processOffline() function, 44
Programming the Mobile Web (Firtman), 16
push technology, 96
Pusher, 96
Python Twisted (WebSocket framework), 106

R

racy behavior, 114
reddit, 5
rotating transition, 29–30
    on Android devices, 29

About the Author

Wesley Hales is a User Interface architect from Atlanta, GA. He has been involved in UI and User Experience roles for over a decade in both startup and enterprise environments. Wesley co-founded several enterprise frameworks during his 4.5 years at JBoss by Red Hat (including the JBoss Portlet Bridge and AeroGear projects) and also served as a co-founder of the recently acquired startup, InstaOps. Overall, Wesley enjoys creating world-class user interfaces and experiences that people fall in love with. You can see him speak at the occasional conference, read his posts on *wesleyhales.com*, or follow him on Twitter @wesleyhales.

Colophon

The animal on the cover of *HTML5 and JavaScript Web Apps* is the cornetfish of the genus *Fistularia*. Because of its long and thin shape, it is also called the flutemouth, tabacco pipe fish, and the rifle fish. There are four species of cornetfish, which can be found in the Atlantic, western Pacific, and Indian oceans. They thrive in coral reefs, coastal waters, sea grasses, and sand flats.

The cornetfish is a thin fish with a long snout and small mouth. They can grow up to 200 centimeters in length. It has a distinct filament near the end of the backbone that also contributes to its length. They feed on other fish, small crustaceans, and invertebrates.

The cover image is from Wood's *Animate Creations*. The cover font is Adobe ITC Garamond. The text font is Minion Pro by Robert Slimbach; the heading font is Myriad Pro by Robert Slimbach and Carol Twombly; and the code font is UbuntuMono by Dalton Maag.

Get even more for your money.

Join the O'Reilly Community, and register the O'Reilly books you own. It's free, and you'll get:

- $4.99 ebook upgrade offer
- 40% upgrade offer on O'Reilly print books
- Membership discounts on books and events
- Free lifetime updates to ebooks and videos
- Multiple ebook formats, DRM FREE
- Participation in the O'Reilly community
- Newsletters
- Account management
- 100% Satisfaction Guarantee

Signing up is easy:

1. Go to: oreilly.com/go/register
2. Create an O'Reilly login.
3. Provide your address.
4. Register your books.

Note: English-language books only

To order books online:
oreilly.com/store

For questions about products or an order:
orders@oreilly.com

To sign up to get topic-specific email announcements and/or news about upcoming books, conferences, special offers, and new technologies:
elists@oreilly.com

For technical questions about book content:
booktech@oreilly.com

To submit new book proposals to our editors:
proposals@oreilly.com

O'Reilly books are available in multiple DRM-free ebook formats. For more information:
oreilly.com/ebooks

Spreading the knowledge of innovators   oreilly.com

Have it your way.